T0266649

9 STEPS
TO FINANCIAL FREEDOM

Also by Dr. John Demartini

The Gratitude Effect
The Productivity Factor
The Resilient Mind
The 7 Secret Treasures
Essentials of Emotional Intelligence

9 STEPS TO FINANCIAL FREEDOM

WISDOM, STRATEGIES AND TACTICS FOR ABUNDANT WEALTH

DR. JOHN DEMARTINI

Published 2024 by Gildan Media LLC
aka G&D Media
www.GandDmedia.com

Front cover design by David Rheinhardt of Pyrographx

Interior design by Meghan Day Healey of Story Horse, LLC.

Library of Congress Cataloging-in-Publication Data is available upon request

ISBN: 978-1-7225-0679-7

10 9 8 7 6 5 4 3 2 1

Contents

Contents

Foreword

I n this book, Dr. John Demartini will reveal inspiring insights on how to master the mindset of wise investing and financial wealth building. He will provide effective strategies for creating moneymaking opportunities, outline a step-by-step pathway for amassing a great fortune, and warn you away from immediate gratification, financial speculations, fantasies, distractions, and schemes. This book will help you awaken your inner drive to achieve the financial objectives you desire and deserve.

Introduction

In this book, you're going to explore the topic of financial mastery and how to build financial wealth. It's primarily about the psychology of financial wealth building. You're going to explore how to grow beyond the financial obstacles you may have placed on or around yourself, because financial wealth building has a lot to do with yourself. I can teach you strategies, but the most important component is getting you beyond the limits you place on yourself to follow those strategies. Most people have some interior or unconscious motive which keeps them from financial wealth building. So you're going to spend time on transforming your perceptions of yourself and your relationship with money and financial wealth building to set yourself free.

A little bit about myself: I have been involved in the field human behavior, personal development, business, leadership and self-mastery for over five decades, and I have been actively involved in financial wealth development full-on for over four decades. Prior to that, I was developing my financial wealth, and it just kept growing, but I didn't at first know what to do with it. I realized that I desired to learn significantly more about this subject. I had other knowledgeable individuals also mentor me, and I pushed myself to read and learn as much as I could, because I wanted to be able to manage my own financial wealth and be financially independent. As I was learning the principles and methods of financial wealth building, other people started to see what I was achieving. They started asking me questions, and the process just kept growing up until today.

I'm going to give you financial wealth building strategies, but I'm also going to talk to you about the psychology of financial wealth building, because I'm convinced that's probably the most important component: the mind game of financial wealth building. Although there are many books on how to get financially wealthy, you may not actually do what these books suggest or what is required unless you have a big enough reason or *why,* so I'm going to talk about the mind game and also the why.

Let me begin by defining financial mastery and freedom. You are a financial master that is free when you have managed your financial wealth wisely enough to no longer be its slave. In other words, you have saved and then invested your money in true assets that appreciate in value to such a degree that it is working for you instead of you working for it, and its passive return or income has now exceeded your active income and need to work, although you may wisely choose to continue to work because you love what you do, but no longer because you feel you have to.

According to Hubert Howe Bancroft, author of the great classic *Book of Wealth*, there are two main driving forces for human beings: spiritual and material. The spiritual driving force involves a quest for some degree of equanimity, philanthropy, and immortality. The second force is the material quest for financial freedom. Some ancient philosophers believed that spirit without matter was expressionless, and matter without spirit was motionless. Both were to be empowered and integrated. Most everyone wants to be liberated in their spirit, but they also want to be liberated materially and financially, to have the freedom and options that money and financial freedom can buy. The two intertwine to create a driving force that is both liberating and immortalizing.

This book is not about get-rich-quick schemes; maybe you have been caught by a few of those types of books. In most cases, those actually can get you poor quick. They're not the answer.

Here I'm going to give you a system that's very methodical, strategic, and simple to follow. If you do follow it, it will help you build more lasting financial wealth. But this system or process is as much about building your self-worth, character, and discipline as about your financial wealth strategies per se.

Let's look at what wealth is. *Wealth,* in its original sense, was derived from *weal,* which meant *well-being.* You become a financial master when you as an individual have liberated your life and attained a state of financial well-being, a degree of self-actualization, and the ability to do what you love and love what you do because you love to, not because you have to. Then your *vacation* and *vocation* are in a sense synonymous.

I'd also like to define *money.* Money is simply a means of exchange. It has no moral value. It's not good or bad, right or wrong, positive or negative. It's simply a means of exchanging one individual's value for that of another. You exchange something that's of value for you for something that's of value for somebody else. It allows for a sustainable fair exchange, or complete transaction. Money exchanging is much more efficient than bartering. It can permanently ensure the coincidence of wants.

One time my late wife, Athena, and I were in New York having dinner with Robin Leach, who was best known for his TV program *Lifestyles of the Rich and Famous.* We were discussing the relationship between religion, philosophy, and wealth.

Robin was saying that he had done a segment of *Lifestyles of Rich and Famous* called "Treasures of the Vatican." He got permission to go into the underground chambers and chapels and the areas where they had stored all their art and goods. Robin told me, "John, if the amount of potential financial wealth that's sitting in these football-field-size chambers and the hundreds of chapels—if all the statues, gold, diamonds, jewels, and artwork were distributed equally across the world but somehow kept their current value— every human being would be a multimillionaire. The vastness of equivalent financial wealth is incomprehensible."

I mention this story because sometimes, through religious instruction, you may have been told that it is more blessed to give than to receive. Fortunately or possibly unfortunately, the church acquired financial wealth, power, and control by keeping people ignorant and impoverished precisely by using such one-sided teachings. In case you have a religious strand in your psyche that might be holding you back, thinking that somehow financial wealth is not honorable, that is misleading and erroneous. It is the direct contradiction of what is true.

I'm going to debunk that belief. Actually, it is more blessed to engage in sustainable fair exchange than anything else. Fair exchange is providing a service that's valuable to someone else for a reward of equal value to you. A culture that does not develop sustainable fair exchange is one that stagnates. It does not develop its commerce, art, science, religion, or philosophy and has a tendency to decay. But the culture that masters the art of financial wealth building and sustainable fair exchange is a culture that contributes, expands, and prospers.

The same is true of you as an individual. When you master the laws that govern sustainable fair exchange and financial wealth building, you will more fully contribute to the planet. You will add to the shift in the financial paradigms and the belief systems of humanity.

You are going to accomplish more by shining than shrinking. You're going to be able to do more by expanding your financial wealth than contracting it. You're going to serve more by showing other people what's possible than by buying into somebody who is going to expand at your expense. Let's start now.

Nine Principles of Wealth Building

1. Appreciating money enables it to grow in your life.
2. Your hierarchy of values dictates what you do with your money.
3. Having a cause greater than yourself will inspire you to increase your financial wealth.
4. Valuing yourself by living according to your own true values.
5. If you help other people get what they want, you will get what you want.
6. Financially wealthy people pay themselves first.
7. The wisest way to acquire financial wealth is to have a forced automated and accelerated saving and then investment program.
8. Money goes to where it's most organized.
9. The greater your certainty, the greater your potential for financial wealth building.

Nine Principles of Wealth Building

1. Appreciating money enables it to grow in your life.
2. Your hierarchy of values dictates what you do with your money.
3. Having a cause greater than yourself will inspire you to increase your financial wealth.
4. Valuing yourself by living according to your own true values.
5. If you help other people get what they want, you will get what you want.
6. Financially wealthy people pay themselves first.
7. The wisest way to acquire financial wealth is to have a forced automated and accelerated saving and then investment program.
8. Money goes to where it's most organized.
9. The greater your certainty, the greater your potential for financial wealth building.

1

Appreciating Wealth

I would love to begin by stating some basic principles. First, let's think about appreciation. If you're in a relationship and you don't appreciate the one you're with, does the relationship tend to grow and prosper? No, it tends to decay, doesn't it?

In real estate, something that appreciates grows in value. So the first principle is to appreciate money so it can grow in value in your life, just like any relationship.

If you have in your mind an internal dialogue that says, "I'm not in it for the money," "Money's not important to me," or "Money is not really what counts," you are contradicting your own natural inclination to expand or grow financially.

You will more effectively grow your financial wealth if you truly appreciate it and the opportunities and services it can bring or provide. When your money is used equitably, in sustainable fair exchange, and managed wisely, more money is drawn or given to you, because appreciation of money allows it to grow. It is wise to appreciate it, allow it to come into your life, and appreciate the opportunity to use it and serve with it.

So the first principle is to appreciate money. The more you appreciate it, the more it can appreciate in value in your life.

The Hierarchy of Values

You have a hierarchy of values, a set of priorities, that indicates what is of greatest and least importance to you. Your values originate from your perceptions of what's perceived as missing. If you perceive that you have little to no money, you will seek money. If you perceive you have no relationship, you will seek a relationship. If you perceive you have no sex, you will seek sex. If you perceive you have no children, you will seek children.

In short, whatever you perceive as most missing becomes most important. *Your voids drive your values. Fulfillment* means *filling full* your *mind*, which presumes some emptiness. Similarly, *satiation* and *satisfaction* mean *to fill* something.

You as an individual have a unique hierarchy of values. Imagine that your highest value is being there for your children, and let's say that number seven on your list of values is saving and then investing or building financial wealth. The second you receive your monthly income—whether it's $5,000, $10,000 or $100,000—you will spend it in accordance with the hierarchy of your values. If saving, investing, and financial wealth building are very low on the hierarchy of your values, you will give your children a fantastic education, you'll have a nice house and nice clothes for them, but you probably won't have any money left over for saving and investing.

Your hierarchy of values dictates how you spend or distribute your money. It determines your priorities. If financial wealth building is not near the top (or at least within the top four), you will probably have more month at the end of your money than money at the end of your month. In other words, you'll probably run out of cash before you get around to saving and investing.

Now here's another little portion of the principle around appreciating money. It's not how much you earn or make that counts; it's the hierarchy of values that dictates how you manage it. Let me elaborate on that.

A few years ago, I had the opportunity to consult for a doctor in Florida who generated $6,290,000 in income that year. You probably think that if you earned that much money, you'd be able to save and then invest some portion. But at the end of the year, the gentleman had to borrow $327,000 from a lending institution to pay his taxes.

You're probably thinking, "That guy's an idiot." No: paying taxes was simply very low on his hierarchy of values and saving and investing even lower. At the top of his list of values were fancy cars, travel, fancy homes, extravagant foods and wines, lots of paintings, a yacht, and a great social life. He devalued paying taxes and devalued paying himself, so he was in debt at the end of the year.

It just so happened that this man had an assistant who was being paid around $2,000 a month but was saving $400 a month. She was moving further toward financial independence than he was. Why? She had building financial wealth for her future higher on her value list than her boss did.

As far as financial freedom is concerned, it makes little to no difference how much money you make; it has everything to do with your hierarchy of values and the way you manage your money. The second you make more money, you tend to raise your lifestyle—if lifestyle is more important than financial wealth building. You get a credit card that gives you a bigger amount you can spend, and you take your spending up to the edge again.

Statistically, the majority of people will increase their spending up to the point where they're 10 percent behind and in debt. Instead of saving and then investing 10 percent, they'll be at a debt level of 10 percent on an annual basis, paying off credit cards at high interest rates.

Again, your hierarchy of values dictates your financial destiny. It determines what you appreciate or depreciate. An individual whose highest value is their children has a high appreciation for their children and possibly a lower appreciation for their savings and investments. They'd rather spend that money on their children now than on their financial future. No one is inherently right or wrong for their unique hierarchy of values, but expecting to be financially free with a low value on financial wealth building will probably leave you feeling frustrated and unfulfilled financially. And attempting to live outside your own true hierarchy of values can become self-depreciating and even depressing.

You may find this a shocker: in my experience, if financial wealth building, or saving and then investing money, are not among the top four values in your value system, in all probability, you're not going to be a financially wealthy or financially free individual, because you'll continue to have something else to spend most of your money on first.

I'm not making that right or wrong. It's not that you're bad because you didn't save and then invest your money. But you are not reading this book to learn how to diminish your financial status; you probably would love to grow it, and you're reading this book at least partly for that reason. You probably would love to understand how important financial wealth really is to you. You can finish this book, but if building financial wealth is still low on your value list, you will possibly walk away with little changed. Unless there's a transformation in the placement of financial wealth building on your list of values, there probably won't be a transformation in your financial life.

Let me explain how our hierarchy of values shapes not only our individual agendas but our perceptions of the world. Say a husband and wife are walking in a mall. Let's say the wife's highest value is her children, and let's say her husband's highest value is building his business and his financial wealth.

As they're walking hand in hand, the wife will be paying attention to children's clothes, children's educational materials—everything to do with her children. But her husband is noticing *Forbes* magazine, *Money* magazine, computers—anything that might help his business and income grow. The hierarchy of values of each one determines what they filter out of their environment.

The individual who has financial wealth building at the top of their hierarchy will see financial wealth building opportunities that someone who has it much lower will never even notice. Your hierarchy of values determines how you sense and filter the world and how you decide to act upon it. It also determines how you spend your money, because if your children are at the top of your list of priorities, you're going to spend money on them. If savings and then investing are high in your list of values, you're going to save and then invest. This point is crucial, because a shift in your hierarchy of values will bring about a shift in your financial destiny.

If I were to ask you to total up every dollar you've earned during all the time you have lived on this planet and compare it to your present net worth—which indicates how much you have actually saved and then invested— that will tell you lot about where money is placed on your value list.

According to figures from the Federal Reserve, in 2019 the average American family had $41,600 in savings. And according to Yahoo!finance, only 14 percent of Americans have $100,000 saved for retirement. Nearly 37 percent said they haven't started saving for retirement at all.

Contrast this with an elderly lady who never earned more than $2.50 an hour in any of her two simultaneous held jobs. But she saved and wisely invested 17 percent of her income, and late in life she contributed $10 million to a

charitable organization. Whatever she made, she saved and then invested methodically. That money accumulated and compounded. She also was advantaged by the deferred taxation of the long-term capital gains most of her U.S. stocks provided as they went up over the five decades she invested.

Financial independence has little or nothing to do with how much you make. Actually, it takes about the same amount of time to be financially independent whether you're making $50 an hour, $500 an hour, or $5,000 an hour, because the same science applies.

This is our first principle: appreciating money and financial wealth building. This means putting it higher on your value list, because if it isn't, money and its wealth building advantages are not going to come to you. Whatever you appreciate comes to you. If you appreciate your husband or wife, you have a higher probability of a long-lasting relationship. If you don't, your relationship can decay and you can start all over, just like with your savings and your accumulated investments.

Think of it this way. If you want a job promotion but you don't appreciate or know much about the new position you want, why would you expect to get that promotion and position? If you truly valued it, you would learn as much as possible about it in advance so you are prepared to receive it.

Similarly, if you don't know how to manage your money wisely, why would the world economic system give you more money to manage? When you manage money wisely, more money will show up in your hands to manage. When you manage money poorly, more money will be taken away. To those who have, more is given; to those who haven't, more is taken away. Furthermore, people who appreciate money and financial wealth building tend to think in the long term and put it where it appreciates in value: they buy assets that go up in value. People that don't appreciate money and financial wealth building tend to think in terms of immediate gratification and spend their money on consumables that depreciate in value.

Another point: if I have zero money and all of a sudden I earn and receive $1, my gain is 100 percent: the value of $1. If I have $10 saved and I add $1, that's 10 percent of my wealth. If I have $100 saved and I add $1, it's 1 percent of my wealth. If I have $1 million saved, each individual dollar becomes less and less valuable.

This means you can easily develop a built-in resistance, or reduced drive factor, in your psyche for accumulating additional financial wealth. Every time you earn a dollar, you have a diminishing motivation to earn yet another dollar. Your desire to attain one more dollar can therefore decrease as you accumulate financial wealth. As you accumulate money, your motivation to accumulate still more money goes down—unless your urge or drive to earn more goes up correspondingly.

Many people plateau as soon as they have accumulated a certain amount of money. If their intrinsic drive doesn't increase correspondingly, their financial growth can stagnate. No matter what they do, they don't seem to build up any more accumulated money. Their motivation to earn more declines, and they plateau.

Everybody has a plateau point, which is directly proportionate to the size of your cause to serve and earn and your vision. So here's another principle: unless your drive for building financial wealth is growing faster than your amount of money, you will probably plateau. Now you've got enough to keep you comfortable; you've got enough to take care of your bills and all the items on your value list. You don't have any more reason to earn, receive, or accumulate more money. At that point, in order to continue to build financial wealth, you require a greater driving cause, and the driving power of the cause will be required to grow at a rate greater than the accumulating dollar value of your financial wealth. When an individual has an intrinsic drive or cause, a big enough *why*, the *hows* of acquiring more financial wealth take care of themselves.

Your Life Demonstrates Your Values

If I asked you where financial wealth building and financial freedom is on your value list, you might immediately say that it is higher than it actually is. But your life demonstrates what truly is of value to you. You can't lie about it; you can't fake it; your life speaks too loud. If you have a negative net worth, financial wealth building has probably not been very high on your value list, because whatever you're putting that money into or spending it on instead has been more valuable.

What is your driving financial cause? What are you going to contribute your accumulated money toward? Is it going to be simply for your retirement? For your comfort? Those are relatively small causes.

I knew a lady in Houston, Texas, who was a noted and respected financial broker. At the time, she was in her twenties, and she was averaging between $6,000 and $7,000 take-home net per day. I started working with her; she used me as a mentor. She built her financial wealth up to where it was averaging between $14,000 and $17,000 a day take-home. Then she hit a plateau for a year or two. She said, "I'm sitting in a plateau; do you have any plateau breaking ideas or strategies?"

"Yes," I said, "I have a very meaningful question I am going to ask you. If you had only twenty-four hours to live, what's incomplete in your life—what have you not fulfilled or accomplished that is deeply meaningful and truly important to you?"

She choked up, got a tear in her eye, and mentioned the name of her mother.

"What about your mother?" I asked.

"I feel like she dedicated her working life to and for me, and I haven't contributed back to her as much as I'd love and feel she deserves." Her mother had worked two jobs so her daughter could go to college and achieve and flourish financially.

"What do you feel you would love to do?" I asked.

"I feel like she never got to do many of the actions she stated that she wanted to do. I'd like to contribute back to her."

"What is that?"

She said her mother loved the performing arts—musicals, plays, the opera, the symphony—but had hardly ever been given the chance to see them.

"What would you love to do?"

She started crying. "I'd love to participate in building a performing arts center in Houston for her." It just came out of her heart.

The lady had a lot of financially wealthy clients; she'd already accumulated a few million dollars. She started talking to some people she knew and some of her wealthy clients, and she inspired them to participate in her cause. As a result, there is a great additional Theater Center in downtown Houston.

Once this lady had a cause, her income went up to sometimes $32,000 a day. She pushed herself to new levels, because now she had a greater and more meaningful cause: trying to build this theater center before her mother passed away.

This lady also has a foundation to inspire and educate children. She inspires young children to live their lives to the fullest and tries to help them with achieving their dreams. Because she's already finished the theater, she's gone on to another level, and she's contributed to many other fortunes.

It's a basic law: if you help other people get where they would love to get in life, you get where you would love to get in life. But what is your greater driving cause? If it's just comfort, the second you get comfortable, you'll probably plateau financially.

When your *why* is big enough, your *hows* take care of themselves. The more intensely empowering and inspiring your *why* becomes, the more powerful your financial wealth building potential will be. What's your great *why*? What is your deeply meaningful reason for building financial wealth? If you don't have a big enough reason, you're probably going to get comfortable and plateau. It's not that you don't have the ability or the opportunities for financial wealth building; they're all around you. But without a great enough intrinsic driving factor, you are unlikely to get far.

At this point, I would encourage you to take a pencil and paper or begin a file on your computer or phone and begin compiling an ongoing, comprehensive, written or typed list of truly meaningful reasons for being financially free and wealthy. Maybe it's having enough funds for your grandchildren to go to college. Maybe it's purchasing a great piece of property to develop. Maybe it's creating a park for children or families. Maybe it's retiring and traveling around the world on a yacht, or any combination of these. Just write down what would intrinsically drive or inspire you to accumulate greater financial wealth. Remember, the greater your cause and the greater your intrinsic drive to save and then invest, the higher the probability of financial wealth coming in your life.

Speaking personally, I didn't begin to fully read until I was seventeen, almost eighteen. I was told as a child that I would probably never be able to read, write, or communicate effectively; I had learning disabilities and a speech impediment. So when I finally was able to learn to read (with the help of a great teacher), learning became important to me, because my inner void eventually drove one of my most meaningful values. As a result, learning and teaching are very high on my list of values still to this day.

Also at age eighteen, I had a dream to master my life. To me at that time, mastery meant mastering all areas of my life:

I desired mentally to create original ideas that served humanity and to be a masterful teacher.

I desired to create a global educational business that served ever greater numbers of people around the world.

I desired to become financially independent many times over so I could work because I loved to, not because I had to.

I desired to have a global family and be a citizen of the world, traveling to and living in every country around the world.

I desired to have global social influence and hang out with and befriend great movers and shakers.

I desired to be vital, fit, and youthful, living simply, wisely, and naturally.

I desired to create an inspiring thought movement designed to share greater love and wisdom throughout the world.

All of these objectives have either already been actualized or are being actualized today, and I am more than grateful for the many opportunities that pursuing my mission and these objectives have brought me. As Einstein once stated, exemplification is the greatest teacher.

It was certainly my pursuit of financial mastery that made many of the other of these other objectives come to fruition.

Motivation versus Inspiration

There are two primary drivers of action and function. One is *extrinsic motivation*, and the other is intrinsic motivation, or what I prefer to call *inspiration*. Let me elaborate on the difference.

As we've seen, everyone has a hierarchy of values. When they are being true to their highest values and living according to them, they are spontaneously inspired. Nobody has to discipline them to do what's most important to them. But it becomes more difficult when you're trying to do things that are lower on your value list. In fact, the lower an item or action is on your value list, the more you will require outside motivation to act upon it.

If you meet somebody with a different hierarchy of values and you admire them and put them on a pedestal, perceiving them as some form of authority, you will inject their value systems into your own. This will engender internal conflict, because you're trying to simultaneously live your own value systems as well as theirs. You will require outside motivation to live theirs, but you will only feel inspired from within when you live according to your own highest values. The resulting conflict will cause emotional turmoil or chaos. As a result, knowing yourself—which means knowing your own true highest values—is one of the most stabilizing actions you can take.

People who minimize themselves tend to sacrifice or work for others, so the money tends to go from them to others they value more. Self-aggrandizing people do the opposite, narcissistically feeling that others owe them something. On the one hand, you have an elevated but false self-esteem; on the other hand, an equally false but depressed self-esteem. Those elements together create the more capitalistic haves and the more socialistic have-nots in society.

Sustainable fair exchange is the balance point: you're not narcissistically trying to get something for nothing. Nor are you trying to give something for nothing in a pseudo-altruistic mode. Instead, you're trying to give something for something in fair exchange. Sustainable fair exchange occurs when you are demonstrating true and stable self-worth, when you find and strike a balance between your elevated and depressed false, self-esteem-based personas.

Conversely, when you go out of fair exchange, you either exaggerate or minimize your self-esteem. In either case, you tend to set unreasonable objectives. If you have an inflated view of yourself, you tend to set too high goals in too short a period of time. You think you can do anything. Because this is unrealistic, eventually you come crashing down. Then you beat yourself up and think you can't do anything. In this process, you oscillate around who you really are instead of being in fair exchange with who you are and with others. Fair exchange keeps you poised instead of poisoned; it keeps you in the present instead of living in the past or future.

Billionaire Warren Buffett said that until you can manage your emotions, don't expect to manage money. Emotions cost you money, because they make you think either that you can do something quicker or bigger than you can or that you can't do it at all. Both keep you from being present, objective, and in sustainable fair exchange.

Your List of Screwups

In all probability, you have stored in your subconscious mind, a mental list of actions you think you have done that you thought to be less than ideal, actions that you judged about or within yourself. In fact, I'd love for you to do another little exercise right now.

I suggest that you take a pencil and paper and write down five instances in your life when you think you harshly judged yourself. Now take the one about which you feel the most shame or guilt. Write that down on a separate line, and put two columns underneath it. In one column, write, "How did this serve me?" In the other write, "How did this serve others?" In each column, quickly write down at least ten benefits to you and ten benefits to the specific others involved, directly or indirectly, that came from that one supposed blooper, mistake, or screwup.

As you do this exercise, you will notice that the perceptions of shame and guilt you felt within begin to subside as you list the benefits and you begin to feel, "Actually, that was not such a mistake after all." Write down how this apparent mistake served you and others until you can say, "I'm now actually grateful that I did that. I learned something from it and served others by doing it, and now I can appreciate what I did and move on."

Otherwise, you're carrying previously stored emotional baggage around, which interferes with your feelings of self-worth and your willingness to receive, save, invest, and accumulate money. Work through your apparent screwups and see how they have served you and others. This will raise your self-worth, and the greater your self-worth, the greater your potential financial net worth.

Deserving Your Inheritance

Here's another little exercise to do if you ever receive an inheritance or a sum of money that you weren't expecting. Write down, "What did I do to receive and deserve this?" Here's why: if you do not feel you deserve that money, in a very short period of time you will find that it disappears from your life. You'll give it to a broker who will blow it; you'll buy some consumable that will depreciate in value; you'll end up with a health issue or an accident; or you'll attract some form of financial opportunist. Something will bring you back down to your perceived level of self-worth. The second you can see that you've deserved it, you'll manage it differently, because now you feel you worked for it and deserve receiving it.

Whenever you feel you have received money you didn't earn or deserve, write down why you actually *do* deserve it. What did you actually do to deserve receiving it? Don't stop until you get a tear in your eye and you know exactly why you received that money. When you do, you'll manage it differently and will be able to hold on to it, because someone who works for their money manages it differently than someone who didn't or doesn't feel they did.

Your Money and Your Lifestyle

Here is another exercise that will probably serve as a wakeup call. Again, take a pencil and paper, and at the top of the paper, write your gross annual income: how much you make in a year before taxes. Underneath that, write down your ideal gross annual income. What would you prefer it to be? Be somewhat reasonable. What would you prefer it to be?

Let's say your real current gross annual income is $50,000, but you'd ideally love to make $100,000. Now you have a total of $150,000. Now divide this number by 2, so you come up with $75,000. This represents a midpoint between your current real and ideal incomes.

Right underneath that, write your age. Now add 22 years to it. If you're 20, write down 42. Now take the averaged number you have already come up with—in this case, $75,000—and double it. Now it's $150,000 in 22 years.

Do the same thing again. From age 42, go to age 64. Double the amount of money again, so now you have $300,000. Now let's add another 22 years, and again double the sum; that'd be 86 and $600,000. Then repeat the process again, so you get 108 years, and $1.2 million.

Here I'm using the average inflation rate, which is about 3.2 percent, meaning that the cost of living is going to double approximately every 22 years.

In short, if you take your real income, add it to the ideal, and divide by two, that gives you a reasonable lifestyle objective at a given point in your life: that is, the lifestyle that you say you'd love to live, which is halfway between real and ideal. But would you like to continue to raise your lifestyle throughout your life? Are you on track with saving your money and then investing it a manner that will provide you with that type of lifestyle?

You figure this out by taking the amount required to maintain this lifestyle, and you multiply it times 12. Say you have already decided that you want to live on a $150,000 income per year at age 64. In order to have that, you require at least 12 times that amount in savings and investments, which amounts to $1.8 million. That's because the income on $1.8 million is $153,000. (I'm basing that on an annual interest rate of 8.5 percent, which may be a bit high for some inexperienced investors.)

In short, at age 64, you'd require at least $1.8 million in savings and investments, earning an average of 8.5 percent annually, to be financially free and live off passive income.

Are you on track? Are you saving and investing to be there? If not, you're probably living in a fantasy about where your money's going to be in the future. If you don't have a clear and viable strategy for getting there, the probability that you will is very slim. You may end up relying on Social Security, which is the largest source of income for most average beneficiaries. For 4 in 10 retirees in 2015, it provided at least 50 percent of their income, and for 1 in 7, it provided at least 90 percent of income. But U.S. Social Security benefits are low compared to those of other developed countries, amounting to less than 40 percent of earned income, according to the Center on Budget and Policy Priorities.

I believe you can save and then invest enough money to meet your long-term objectives, but you may be required to first shock yourself into reality and look truthfully at where you are and what it will actually take to obtain your desired level of financial independence. If you are on track to meet those goals, you may be required to put money and financial wealth building higher on your value list, because it's not just going to manifest out of the wind. To have some financial freedom, it takes an understanding of your current reality accompanied by methodical strategies.

Do You Really Value Wealth?

Let me review the principal points that I've made up to here. It is wise:

1. To appreciate the value of money and accumulating financial wealth.
2. To have an intrinsically driving cause or motive force bigger than yourself to drive your financial wealth acquisition.
3. To release shame and guilt, which can make you feel unworthy of receiving and accumulating money.
4. To have a realistic sense of where you are, where you want to go, and how you intend to get there.

It's about breaking through your possible financial fantasy. It's about asking yourself, "Do I truly value financial wealth building?" "Do I truly feel worthy of receiving or acquiring my desired fortune." Because as soon as you do, you're going to be walking through the mall and seeing opportunities you never saw before. Until then, you're probably going to be living in a financial fantasy, like an extremely high percent of the American or other populations.

Of course there are any number of undetermined variables.

The figures I gave above are based on an annual return of 8.5 percent on your investment, but that's merely an average: in some years, you're not going to get 8.5 percent net return; in other years, you're going to get more. Nor do you know how long you're going to live; nobody knows exactly (unless they plan their death). You might stop working at 60, 70, or even 80 and live to age 100.

That means you would probably need still more income to live the same lifestyle.

Financial mastery is a game of mathematics, a game of probabilities. It is also a relative science. There are certain principles, laws, and rules, and if you follow them, you'll get certain outcomes. If you don't, you have a lower probability of getting those outcomes. You will want to have the probabilities in your favor. You want to have so-called luck in your favor, because luck is preparation meeting opportunity.

The higher the value you place on financial wealth building, the more likely you'll follow an effective strategy. If you do, you've got a higher probability of obtaining and retaining financial wealth. If you don't and just think it's going to manifest somehow, you're dealing with much lower probabilities of accumulating your money and obtaining financial freedom.

I've been asked, "Is your financial wealth building program about getting rich quick?" I've replied, "No, it is not about immediate gratification and speculation. It is more about saving and then investing and getting financially independent and wealthy in the long run. In the short run, it's going to *seem* slower than some of the more speculative get-rich-quick gimmicks." But not in the long run.

You may know people who have tried to get rich quick and ended up back where they started. I know a gentleman in Houston, Texas, who has gone after one get-rich-quick scheme after another—from derivative trading to multi-level marketing organizations to real estate venture gimmicks. I've known him for twenty-eight years, and after all that time, he's still in debt. I've just methodically followed a simple strategy and kept saving and then investing. I'm like the tortoise; he was like the hare. Now I'm living financially free and with the lifestyle that he only dreamed about. Patience and reason are virtues.

The Benefits of Wealth

I would hope by now that you are starting to be a bit more inspired about saving your money, investing, and building your financial fortune. Now let's look at some additional advantages or benefits of building financial wealth.

There is power in accumulating financial assets, or wealth. In fact, there are seven primary powers in life, and building financial wealth can enhance the empowerment of any or all of them:

1. Your spiritual power: having an inspired mission or meaningful spiritual cause or something to which you're dedicating your energies and possibly your life. Building financial wealth can allow you to more effectively fulfill your most inspired mission.

2. Your mental power: awakening your innovative, creative original thinking, and genius or mental faculties in a way that inspires and serves or contributes to humanity. Building financial wealth can allow you to more easily have the time or resources for creative thinking and innovation.

3. Your vocational power: the power of building a great and powerful business, like Amazon, Microsoft, or Oracle, which serves ever greater numbers of people in a sustainable fair exchange manner. Building financial wealth can allow you to more effectively build a more viable business enterprise.

4. Your financial power: your financial freedom, or your power of building sustainable financial wealth. Individuals with vast fortunes can influence millions and contribute philanthropically. Building financial wealth can allow you to keep compounding your assets for further financial accumulation or philanthropic objectives.

5. Your familial power: the stability of a family, lineage, or dynasty, built through equitable and respectful dialogue, love, and intimacy. Building financial wealth can allow you to upgrade your family education, position, standards, and legacy.

6. Your social power: How many people are in your social network? How many people do you lead, influence, or make a difference in the lives of? Building financial wealth can allow you to contribute to more people and have greater opportunities and more influential associations.

7. Your physical power: beauty, vitality, strength. Very fit, handsome, or beautiful individuals have power. They can stop traffic by walking across the street or draw crowds at stadiums. Physically talented sports Olympians have power. Building financial wealth can elevate your health care standards, your environment, and potential levels of fitness training.

If you have someone that's got an inspired mission or a spiritual calling, mental genius, an empowered business, a vast fortune, a stable family, and social connections, and is extremely fit, handsome, or beautiful, you have someone who's very powerful, don't you?

Another advantage or benefit is that financially wealthy people tend to live longer. Remember, the etymology of the word *wealth* is derived from *weal,* which means wellness and well-being. That's been shown statistically. Wealthier individuals and nations are able to have (if desired) higher quality dietary and nutritional standards. They can exercise more and can more effectively take care of themselves. Wealthier nations have higher longevity rates.

Another benefit of becoming financially wealthy is that it provides greater numbers of options, or more freedom of choice. If I have $1 billion, I can decide whether I want to have dinner in Sydney or St. Petersburg and can have my own organic, naturally grown foods chef at my beck and call.

Another important point: every time I add another few zeros to my net worth and accumulated wealth, the more people want to buy me food or other things. It's almost as if accumulating financial wealth attracts more opportunities for building even more financial wealth.

2

The Power of Self-Talk

I would love to take a moment to emphasize the importance of your internal dialogue, or self-talk. When I was seventeen, a very wise elderly man told me to say to myself one statement or affirmation every single day for the rest of my life, and it would change the course of my life.

At the time I was a high-school dropout, a long-haired hippie, living on the north shore of Oahu, surfing every day. I had never read a book from cover to cover, because I had learning disabilities, dyslexia, and a speech impediment. But the night I met this man, I experienced an inspiring vision or dream during his guided-imagery alpha meditation. In it, I was a great and inspiring teacher and philosopher who traveled the world.

After that evening, I had the opportunity to study with this man each morning for three weeks. On my last day I ever saw him, I told him that I didn't know how I could ever live that vision or dream, because I didn't know how to read or speak effectively.

The wise old gentleman said, "That's not a problem. Just say this one statement every single day for the rest of your life, and never miss a day. Say it every single day; never miss a day until the cells of your body tingle with it. The second they do, so will the world."

"What's that?"

"Say, *I am a genius, and I apply my wisdom.*"

He made me say it over and over until I felt it. Two years later, I had returned to school in Texas, learned how to read, began practicing speaking, I was at the top of my class in college, and was tutoring people in yoga, meditation, math and whatever else I was learning.

Every single day, multiple times, I was saying, *I'm a genius, and I apply my wisdom. I'm a master reader: whatever I read, I retain. I have a photographic mind. Whatever is truly important to me, I retain for life,* and that internal dialogue shifted my life. I used another affirmation: *the universe is my playground, the world is my home, every country is another room in the house, and every city is another platform to share my heart and soul,* because I dreamed about setting foot on every country on the face of the earth and teaching.

Now, after fifty-one years of saying those statements and many others daily, I have been fortunate enough to teach, speak, research, and write in over 150 countries on all seven continents and in over 2,000 cities across the globe.

In 2001, I purchased an apartment on a ship called *The World,* which travels all over the world and goes to nearly every country and allows me to have fortunate and adventurous explorations and educational experiences like no other home. So I realized that affirmation: even the name of the ship matched the internal dialogues I have repeated. What you say to yourself does impact your destiny.

Are You Saying What You Would Love to Hear?

You have time to talk to yourself; in fact, you are doing it whether you are aware of it or not, or like it or not. But you may not be saying what you would truly love to hear. You may not be fully taking command of your internal dialogue. You may be filling your mind with internal dialogues or statements that other people are saying instead of deciding what you want to say and saying, commanding, and demanding it. If you don't fill your mind with exactly what you would love, your mind is likely to get filled with what you don't.

When your mind starts wandering and worrying, fill it with what you would love instead. If you don't plant flowers in the garden of your mind, you will forever be pulling weeds. Your highest value-driven purpose and innermost dominant thought will determine your destiny, and they in turn will be based on what is truly intrinsically valuable and of highest priority on your hierarchy of values. Your hierarchy of values determines what you think about, what you visualize, and what you talk about and affirm. If you think, visualize, and affirm what you would love, you increase the probability that it will occur, because your human intention is creative in nature. You have the power in your mind to manifest what you envisage and declare.

Your innermost dominant thought becomes your outer-most tangible reality.

How to Use Your Self-Talk

The next step is clarifying and applying your daily self-talk or internal affirmations. It is wise to take command of what you say to yourself daily, because if you don't, somebody else, possibly less financially savvy, can and probably will.

What would love to say to yourself financially? How would you love your financial life to be? I suggest that you write down at least five statements that you'd love to say to yourself in regard to your actions concerning financial wealth building. For example:

- I am a diligent methodical saver and value investor, on my way to being a multimillionaire.
- I'm a multimillionaire money magnet: whatever I do or wherever I go, I keep running into ever greater opportunities to serve, earn, and wisely invest more, because that is now higher on my value list.
- I'm at the right place at the right time to meet the right people to make the right deal to grow my financial wealth.
- No matter what happens, I turn it into a great financial opportunity that makes me even more prosperous and financially savvy.
- I save and invest my money wisely for short-term, midterm, long-term, lifetime, and beyond lifetime goals that serve myself and others fairly and sustainably across the world.

- I pass by foolish, immediate gratifying, get-rich-quick schemes and choose wiser, long-term financial wealth building objectives and strategies.
- I automate and periodically accelerate my weekly saving and investing routines so my impulsive or instinctive emotions do not distract me from my long-term financial objectives.

These are just some suggestions, but I recommend writing down at least five additional statements concerning your financial strategy actions that you'd love to say to yourself every day—and say them every day. Make it a part of your day. Let them be a checkup from the neck up. Declare exactly how you would love your financial life to be. Just make sure they are congruent with your highest values (after you have elevated financial wealth building on your list of values).

The Pillars of Wealth

The next step is *feeling*. There are four magical feelings that draw money to you: gratitude, love, inspiration, and enthusiasm. Those are the four cardinal pillars of financial wealth building.

When you have a balanced mind and you're grateful, your heart opens: gratitude is the key that opens up the gateway of the heart. When your heart opens, you feel love. When you feel love, your mind is clear, and you become inspired. When you're inspired, your body becomes intrinsically enthusiastic in its actions.

If you have a career that you love and are grateful for, more opportunities will come to you to accumulate financial wealth. I've developed a relatively high degree of financial wealth because I love what I'm doing. I'm grateful for the opportunity to do it each day, I'm inspired by it, and I enthusiastically do it day after day. This has allowed me to serve millions of people and become highly rewarded financially.

Here's another affirmation: *I'm grateful. I'm loving. I'm inspired. I'm enthusiastic.* Say you're selling a product. If you feel inspired about selling it and are grateful for the opportunity to serve the customer with it, your business grows. In fact, with those four feelings—gratitude, love, inspiration, and enthusiasm—it's nearly impossible to stop your business from growing.

Every day, it's wise to write down a list of the experiences and opportunities you are truly grateful for—a "count your blessings" list. When I was about four years old, my mother taught me to count my blessings, because people who are grateful for what they have will receive and experience more to be grateful for.

On my computer, I have my multivolume *State of My Mission* book, composed of thirty-five files or volumes, including an extensive list of about 100,000 experiences and opportunities for which I am grateful, and I'm adding to that list daily. I call it my "blessings list," or "daily gratitude journal." It includes thousands of opportunities that have come to me that I previously set as priority objectives (or wasn't even expecting) that came true. "I had the opportunity to have dinner with so-and-so. I had the opportunity to speak at this location, to sell this new book in this new language."

It's helpful to keep a daily list of blessings in order to train your mind to be grateful. Gratitude opens up the gateway of the heart, allows love to shine out from it, and clears the mind for inspiration, enthusiasm, and financial wealth.

In the 1990s, Fidelity stock market investor Peter Lynch said that after narrowing down his potential stock selections technically and quantitatively, he would travel to visit the flagship offices of the selected companies to see if the executives and employees were grateful for their jobs, loving what they did, inspired by the leader of the company and its mission and vision, working enthusiastically, and having certainty in their skills and present. If they were, it added points to his stock selection process, since it showed an engaged team of experts, which provided a comparative advantage in the market.

The Plan of Action

The next step is a plan of action. How are you going to accomplish what you desire financially? How much are you going to save, and then invest and how frequent? Where are you going to invest it? In other words, how exactly do you intend to manifest your intended financial fortune or wealth?

You will require a strategy as well as the discipline to follow or act on it. You will want to prioritize your actions and take those actions steps that are of the highest priority. You will want to get feedback from your life. On a daily basis, you will want to ask, what worked and what didn't work financially today? What's allowed me to move forward on my financial wealth building objectives, and what didn't? You will want to learn from your experience; otherwise, you will keep repeating the same activities. What worked and what didn't work? Then act on what worked.

One wise and simple way to acquire financial freedom and wealth is to implement a forced automatic and accelerated savings and investment program: you automatically send part of your earned paycheck or income to a separate savings and then investment account. There's no emotion involved; it's just electronically and automatically done. If you do that, magic begins to occur, because the financial investment world is waiting for you to declare your worth and commit to your action. The second you demonstrate that you believe you are worth taking this committed action and you begin to value yourself, people will help you receive that money. When you begin to value yourself, so do others. If you're waiting for others to declare your worth, you'll be waiting for eternity. When you begin to manage money wisely, you begin to receive more money to manage. Money circulates through the economy for those who value themselves and money most.

The formula of financial manifestation could be summarized as follows: awakening and clearly defining your highest value driven purpose for building your financial wealth and freedom. When the why is big enough, the hows will take care of themselves. A great purpose and cause can catalyze a great fortune. When you have enough meaningful and inspiring reasons for building financial wealth, you will do it.

Think about building financial wealth by thinking about the income generating services, management, savings, and investment strategies to achieve it.

Visualizing yourself doing the highest priority action steps that will achieve your goal of building financial wealth and freedom.

Affirming to yourself the daily highest priority action steps that will achieve your goal of building financial wealth and freedom.

Feeling within yourself the gratitude, love, inspiration, and enthusiasm for achieving your goal of building financial wealth and freedom.

Taking spontaneous action toward achieving your objective. Write down exactly how you intend to acquire and manage your accumulated assets—what you will do with them in space and time. Also write down the benefits of accumulating financial wealth and serving yourself and others with it. In fact, I suggest that you write down 100 benefits of accomplishing what you seek. When you feel deserving of building financial wealth and you are thankful for the opportunities that emerge along the way, you will increase the probability of manifesting it. These few steps act like a formula that will assist you in earning, saving, investing, accumulating assets, and achieving financial freedom.

Also, when you commit yourself to an automated saving and investing strategy and accelerate these actions, you initiate a chain reaction of ever greater financial opportunities. By doing so, you are in a sense declaring that you are already worth whatever you are committing. The world around you is waiting for you to make your financial declaration, so you will receive the corresponding opportunities to help you fulfill the reality to which you are now committed. This will also make you see your financial possibilities and opportunities more clearly.

As you begin to accelerate your savings and investments, it is wise to run or calculate quarterly projections: where will you be in one, five, ten, twenty, thirty, forty, at even fifty years if you continue investing a progressive amount of money into quality assets. Once you do, your vision of what is financially possible will expand. What you initially think you are capable of achieving (like being a millionaire) will seem just a starting point. You will begin to realize that being a multimillionaire, billionaire, and possibly even beyond, is also achievable.

I started with saving only $200 a month. Three months later, I raised it to $300 a month. Three months later, I raised it to $500 a month. Three months later, I raised it to $750 a month. Three months later, I raised it to $1,000 a month. I ran a projection of where I would be in one year, five years, and each decade thereafter if I continued saving and investing at that amount. At first, I realized I could be a millionaire in 34 years at that rate. I continued following the forced accelerated saving and investing technique. I added 10 percent extra every quarter, so it became $1,100 a month, then $1,210 a month, then $1,331 a month, then $1,464 a month, then $1,510 a month. Each quarter, I would run another projection, and it revealed that I had reduced the time until I had accumulated my first $1 million by 10 percent each quarter. So 34 years went to about 31 years, then 28 years, then about 25 years, then 23 years, 21 years, 18 years, to just around the corner, to finally being achieved. As I accelerated my quarterly savings and investments every two years, the amount I invested kept doubling. That, in addition to compound interest, started to allow my nest egg to accumulate more rapidly.

Then whenever I finished paying my student loan and later another loan off, I kept adding that monthly loan payment to my monthly investment payments. Soon I was saving and investing $2,000, $4,000, $8,000, $16,000, $32,000, $64,000, $128,000, and eventually $256,000 a month and more. My vision of what was possible kept increasing. It was not so much the amount as the habit and discipline in continuing to increase it that started to work its magic of magnetizing greater financial income generating opportunities.

What Will You Do with Wealth?

Here's another suggestion: take the amount of money that you would love to accumulate; let's say $10 million (or maybe much, much more). It's useful to write down what you're going to do with that $10 million. How will it be actually allocated into various assets? If you don't know what you would actually do with this amount, why would you expect to have the actions, experience, and opportunities that will provide you with it? (If you don't know what to do with a job promotion, why would a company give you that promotion?) What are you going to do with $10 million? How is your money going to be allocated and structured? How and where is it going to be saved and then invested? What simple, but fulfilling and quality lifestyle are you going to have and gradually scale up to?

It's also wise to create pictures of how your life is going to look and be when you attain or exceed your magic figure of true financial freedom. That's why I recommend interviewing multimillionaires: they'll give you an idea of how they structure their lives and how they built their financial fortune. If you associate with multimillionaires or billionaires, you might find their ideas meaningful and expanding. The people you associate with can influence your ideas, opportunities, and outcomes.

Another action worthy of taking is to ask yourself, "What did I do or what am I doing to deserve $10 million?" You start an ongoing list of the services and value you provide to others. The more you value yourself and your actions of service, the more the world of others will.

Your Source of Income

Next principle: what's your inspiring source of income? What's your source of money that is going to be dedicated to building your financial wealth? A number of years ago, I had an opportunity to do a television program, and I needed to raise some money. I needed to raise $80,000, but I didn't want to take it from my own savings. I wanted to disperse some of the potential risk of the show's outcome.

I was inspired by this idea for a TV show, and I sensed I was going to get a good return from it. So I called some of my friends and asked if they'd like to participate. I guaranteed them a 15 percent annual return for the first year. At the time, the average annual return in the market was about 7 to 8 percent. I said, "If you want to invest some money—whatever you want—I will sign a promissory note: I will give you an extra 15 percent one year from now." In forty-five minutes, I had $75,000, just from getting on the telephone. I was enthused, I was doing something I loved, I was inspired, I was grateful, so I had no problem acquiring the money. I paid the investors back within four months. I could have used a lending institution and paid a smaller percentage for the money, but that would not share the opportunity with my friends.

When you have something you truly believe in that truly has potential for a great return, money is abundant. This form of money could be called credit or credibility.

At another point in time, I had the opportunity to work with the originator and manager of a global hedge fund in New York. It was at a high level of finance that I hadn't dealt with yet, but the individual still wanted my opinion on a certain portion of the plan. The organizer knew me and said, "I'd like you to read the fund management plan and give us your ideas about it. See if you can see any problems."

That took me to another level of learning about and earning money, because they were planning on dealing with billions of dollars in a global hedge fund. This man, who was thirty-six years old, took $2 million from his investments, went to Harvard University, and got an economist there to help him design a plan for his global hedge fund. It took him two years to put this business and fund management plan together and get the kinks worked out.

This man opened up the hedge fund and had $100 million the first week and well over $1 billion in three months. This led me to another realization: when you put your financial house in order and offer true potential value and return, money comes to it. Similarly, when you have a plan of action that people feel is going to give them a fair and substantial return, money comes to it as well. This man spent two years concentrating on something so valuable that billions of dollars were invested into it, and he took his 2–3 percent off the top off the fund's profits.

In short, there's never a lack of money. There's simply a quality, viable, and profitable idea that hasn't been crystallized, refined, and packaged in such a way that it's valuable enough for somebody to offer it and others to invest in it. The greater the service and profits you provide, the more the money you will have access to.

The Attraction of Organization

I consulted for another company in Florida, which provided a laser treatment for skin to enhance beauty. The originator spent about two to three years designing and polishing the original concept and went on to build a highly profitably franchise across the U.S. He concentrated on what he knew would be a winning system, and he and his colleagues opened many franchises, each of which yielded him an average of $30,000 a month. He and his franchisees opened over sixty franchise locations in the first three years. Of course, he spent two or three years refining and structuring the business in order to get his company moving and growing even more efficiently.

When you have organized knowledge and a clear intent of serving people in a way that earns ever greater income, you are committed to building financial wealth, and your plan is structured in such a way that it's a clear and definite service in the eyes of the customer, there's no end to the money that's available.

This leads to the next principle: *money goes to where it's organized most.* Let me give you an example. Say there are three financial investment advisors, and you'd like to choose the one you'd like to give your life savings to, for investment purposes.

You go to the first advisor and ask, "What would you do with my money?" He replies, "I don't know yet; I'll have to think about that. I may put some into the stock market. I may put some into bond markets. I may put some into cash, maybe some real estate."

You go to the next advisor and ask what he would do with your money. He says, "Initially I'm going to be conservative with it. I'll put it into a money market account, get you a few percent, and leave it there to make sure you're secure until I decide what is best for you."

Finally you go to the third advisor. He says, "The first thing we're going to do, before I take a dollar out of your pocket, is sit down with you and find out who you are, what you're about, what you're dedicated to: your values, your risk tolerance, and your time horizons. Then I want to design a plan with you that will make sure you achieve your primary financial intentions and objectives. That may take us a period of time, but once it's done, you'll be financially provided for for the rest of your life and be financially free."

Which advisor would you choose? Probably the third one. Why? Because there's more order, structure, and knowledge suggested and offered, and it includes a team effort with your intentions and their guidance.

Organized knowledge has power, so it is wise to put your financial house in order. You will want to organize your financial house and objectives, because the more organized you are in your finances, the more money will come to you. Money circulates in the economy from those with the least financial order to those with the most.

Once my wife and I were in New York, having dinner on 67th Street and Park Avenue in the home of a wealthy gentleman who was CEO of a very large corporation. We arrived a little bit early, and I was looking at his library while we were waiting for him to finish a meeting in Germany.

He had a large, beautiful library. I saw one area, which was about six by eight feet, and it was filled with beautiful leather folders. I peeked inside a few of them, and I was amazed, because these folders contained dossiers on every single asset this man held. The folders would hold pictures of every individual artwork, along with a purchase receipt, an appraisal, and an insurance policy. All of his financial assets were organized and regularly updated.

When this gentleman came into the room, I said, "You're the most financially organized guy I've ever seen."

"Yes," he replied. "If somebody were to steal something, my insurance policy would cover it, and I'd make money on that too. Organized money makes more money."

So guess what I did when I got back to my office? I took every single asset I had, put a folder together, and did exactly what he did. And I knew to the penny where I was financially.

If you don't know where you are or where you're going and you don't have a plan to get there, you will probably be one of the 99 percenters, not the 1 percenters. Whereas people who know where they are and where they're going and have a strategy to get there will more likely achieve it. People who manage money wisely end up with more money to manage.

In short, *the greater your financial certainty, the greater your financial wealth potential*. You don't need to gamble or speculate to be wealthy, but you do require a well thought out plan or structure. So it's wise to put your financial house in order and find out exactly every asset you have. You will blow your mind, because you may find that you have assets you didn't even know about. You may get a fair appraisal and find out that some of your art, and possibly other assets, are more valuable than you thought.

Of course, today you can list all these assets on a computer. At any rate, put your financial house in order. List all your current assets and your current liabilities, and find out your current net worth. It is wise to know your current net worth, to know where you're standing today before you can plan for tomorrow. It's useful to decide what lifestyle you want and when and to know where you are before you can make a plan to get where you want. Failing to plan is planning to fail.

I know some of this is basic, but the basics are what build sound financial wealth. Wall Street institutions and their many market analysts, money managers, traders, and brokers may want you to believe it is complex so they can acquire your assets to manage, but as Warren Buffett's late associate Charlie Munger once stated (and I have individually confirmed), it is simpler than Wall Street wants you to believe.

Not long ago a gentleman said to me, "I went to your seminar, and I want to know, do you have an advanced program?"

"Did you do what I taught you in the first seminar?"

"Well, partly."

"Why do you think you're ready for an advanced seminar when you haven't done the basics?" If you go online for an Uber but you don't know where you are or where you are going, Uber cannot easily assist you.

Your Lifetime Rate of Savings

Here's another exercise: estimate how much you've earned over the course of your life. Write that figure down, and underneath it write down your current net worth. Then determine the percentage you've saved all your life. If it's above about 4 percent, you're above average; money is obviously higher on your list of values. If it's under about 4 percent, money hasn't been a focus; other activities or things have obviously been more important to you.

Here I'm talking about your net worth. That can include equity in your company, stock shares, rental properties, other real estate holdings, fine art, commodities, money market accounts, house, and your car. Your net worth constitutes your savings and investments right now. That's what you've got in your possession that you could liquidate if necessary.

Increasing Your Earnings

To increase your savings and then your appreciating asset investments, it will be wise to increase your earnings. There are two basic ways of accomplishing this: generating more business or keeping the same amount of business and lowering your costs or overhead. Those who value building financial wealth will keep focusing on those two areas and work at doing both. They're constantly trying to maximize their margin, savings, investments and their returns.

Some people may say they're on a fixed income. If you're on a fixed income but you follow my instructions and begin to build some savings and financial investment assets, in all probability within either months or two to three years, you won't be on a fixed income anymore. You will probably become more entrepreneurial and will consider opening your own company to reduce your taxes and raise your income and return on your efforts.

If you are working for somebody else, there are certainly many ways of negotiating more. Some years ago, a lady from Toronto came to a financial wealth building program of mine. She was a high-school teacher, and she was making about $37,000 a year. She said, "I realize that at this rate, I'm not even remotely going to live what I dream about economically unless I marry a wealthy guy," and she didn't want to be dependent upon a man. "I don't know how to get out of this situation."

A fixed income is often a result of a fixed mindset. That's sometimes all it is. So we brainstormed. I said, "Why don't I come and do a talk at the school you teach at? I'll come and inspire the students."

From this she started a new paradigm for teaching. She began inviting other individuals and professional speakers who were already noted and respected high achievers to come to her school and share their life achievement stories. She created a whole new teaching system for her school and then for others. She was inspired. She networked with these high-profile people and started inviting more of them to speak. This gave her a greater and more meaningful cause than just herself. In the meantime, she started consulting and mentoring not only kids but teachers, faculty, administrators, and principals and got paid for it.

She came up with some more strategies, and she invited many more speakers to come. Her extra efforts of making a difference in the students' lives were noticed by the leaders of the school and eventually some other school leaders in that region, because the overall productivity and education level of that school had suddenly gone up. The students were achieving greater academic outcomes because they were inspired by true leaders. Remember, exemplification is the greatest teacher.

This teacher received an opportunity to head up a new division in the educational system, at a higher salary. In addition, she started consulting and speaking on the side for other educational systems. Six to seven years later, she signed a contract for $100,000 for one month's work and made over $1 million that year. She published a series of books in which she shared some of her stories. Now this woman has gone on to do educational, corporate, and professional performance coaching and speaking. She is getting paid much more than she ever did as a secondary school teacher and is financially independent.

A fixed income can mean a fixed mind. A fixed mind can mean that you haven't stopped and asked yourself, "What other assets, skills, or talents do I possess that could be of value or service to other people, that can earn me an amazing living, that would be inspiring to me, that I can't wait to get up in the morning and do?"

Lowering Overhead

A way to lower overhead and other costs so there is more to invest is to ask yourself, "What are the 20 percent of the actions that I'm doing that give me 80 percent of my results?" The late management consultant Joseph Juran demonstrated that 80 percent of your results come from 20 percent of your activities. It's wise to find out what those are. Although you may be thinking that you've heard this before, the question is, have you fully and consistently applied it?

I applied this rule to the selection of my clients. I prioritized them and found the ones that provided me with the most financial return and overall fulfillment for the least amount of effort versus the ones that gave me the least return and satisfaction for the most amount of effort. I concentrated more on the former and less on the latter. My business went up. I did the same again and again each quarter. I just kept prioritizing, like a tree that grows to the sun: it releases and sheds less viable branches. Releasing lower priority actions and interactions helps you grow new branches. If you're holding on to what you've been doing, you're going to keep getting the same results.

If you don't value your time or yourself, don't expect others to value you. Financially wealthy people put a high value on themselves and their time. They use it most effectively on what most inspires them, and they shed lower priority, less productive distractions.

Sharing what you have to offer others in terms of their highest values assist them in valuing you. But because there is a whole spectrum of values from one extreme to the other in society, you are not likely to fulfill the highest values and needs of 100 percent of the people. Your services will resonate with some, and not with others. Some will consider you to be inexpensive and others expensive.

If you honorably release less resonant individuals, they may initially and temporarily think you're arrogant, expensive, or greedy. But this is probably because they do not value you or understand why you are wisely being more selective.

If you surround yourself with people who don't resonate with or appreciate your products, services, or ideas and think you're expensive or greedy, it may be time to shed those branches and grow to your next level. If you hold on to them instead of moving on, you're gravitating instead of radiating and expanding. By doing so, you could be giving them permission to do the same in their life.

If you want to build financial wealth, you can make a list of every specific action you do in a day and put a dollar value of how much it produces per hour next to it. Factor whatever actions you may do over a three-month period, and be inclusive. That was a real eye-opener for me when I first did this at age twenty-seven. I realized that I was doing some unproductive actions in my clinical practice that were netting me zero dollars and other, more productive actions that were netting me tens, hundreds, or thousands of dollars per hour. As long as I was spending time doing low-priority and low-producing actions, I was devaluing my time and holding my business and myself back financially. Now I basically do four things: I professionally speak, research, write, and travel the world. I've delegated everything else away to specialists. I only do what I love.

It's wise to make a list of all of your activities, determine the value per minute or hour for each of them, prioritize them according to their productivity, and then delegate the lower-priority items to somebody who would be inspired by and more skilled at doing them. Streamline, prioritize, delegate.

When I started my chiropractic practice in 1982, I was doing almost all of the tasks. Then I found out that I produced the most income per minute speaking to audiences who were potential new patients, training new doctors in clinical procedures, and adjusting patients. I started to do presentations to inspire new patients, and I became quite proficient at that. If I spoke at a business networking, corporate function, or conference and I were to generate five to eight new patients out of it (which was average), each of whom would generate an average of $2,500 in services, I could generate $12,500–$20,000 doing a half hour to one hour presentation. As a result, it was more effective and efficient for me to speak for an hour and delegate all other actions to my hired doctors or specialized staff.

The idea is to prioritize your daily activities. If there's any possibility that you could hire somebody to do a given activity at less cost than you can earn yourself elsewhere, it's wiser to hire somebody to do that. If you charge hundreds or thousands of dollars per hour for your services and can get some specialist to do your bookkeeping, or other administrative activities for tens of dollars per hour, it makes more sense to do that rather than doing your own bookkeeping and administrative duties.

I was working with a gentleman in Dallas who was working for a company. He was on a fixed income. He asked his boss for a raise. His boss said there wouldn't be any raises for a year or two. Furthermore, the boss said, there was no way that this gentleman could do outside work; if he did, he would be fired due to conflict of interest.

So we sat down for an hour and a half and worked out what he could do that's valuable to him in such a way that he would either have freedom to go out and do other income generating jobs or earn greater income. He put together a proposal. He didn't receive a raise, but after a bit of negotiating he was allowed the opportunity to do another activity that could earn extra income. His boss agreed that he could do it as long as it didn't interfere with his current production or the company's clients.

The gentleman asked whether he could do this particular project, increasing his regular production by 10 percent a year, and still be allowed to continue. He negotiated the freedom to do consulting on the side as long as he increased his production for the company he was working for. He went from fixed thinking to opening up a doorway to freelance consulting outside his regular hours. Eventually his intention was to turn the company that he was working for into one of his many clients, so he could write off his business expenses and end up with new clients and more income. This is exactly what he was able to do.

Unless you more efficiently manage the use of your time, it's not realistic to expect to receive more money to manage. If you don't spend your energy on high-priority actions, it will be spent on low-priority actions. When I was in practice, I realized that if I had what initially appeared to be idle or down time, I started worrying, wondering, and doubting. So I made a list of high priority productive actions that I could do to build my business while I had any so-called idle time: calling clients, writing thank-yous, strategizing, rereading my goals, reviewing patient files, practicing procedures. As a result, I didn't have idle time; I had high-priority tasks that produced more clients or added to providing more skillful clinical care.

It's sensible to fill your day and take command of it with productive and high priority actions. Whoever has the agenda in a meeting rules the meeting, and your life's highest priorities and most productive actions can be your agenda. If you don't have your daily agenda mapped out, somebody else will slide their agenda into your time. Unless their value on helping you build your financial wealth is greater than yours, your own value on financial wealth building is probably going to drop instead of grow.

Associate with Wealth

This leads me to the next principle: I encourage you to consider associating with financially wealthy and highly integral people, find out what's common to them, and let their ideas rub off on you. It's valuable to associate with people with vision, dreams, goals, and objectives—people that are integrally building financial wealth through sustainable fair exchange and contributing to the planet. If you associate with quality multimillionaires, you will probably end up one; if you associate with billionaires, you could possibly end up one.

It's wise to prioritize and target the people you'd love to associate and resonate with. Whom would you love to resonate with? If you have ten dollars saved, you get ten-dollar ideas and ten-dollar opportunities. If you have one hundred dollars saved, you get hundred-dollar ideas and hundred-dollar opportunities. If you have a thousand dollars saved, you get thousand-dollar ideas and thousand-dollar opportunities. If you have a million dollars saved and invested, guess what happens? Million-dollar ideas and opportunities start to come to you; you get ideas about how to make an extra million. You get new opportunities given to you. You start having opportunities to hang out with more financially wealthy individuals, which can escalate the growth of your financial wealth.

I suggest that you make a list of the people you'd love to meet, the people you'd love to resonate with. You have nothing to lose by calling them up and asking, "I'd like to take you to dinner." You may pay a hundred or more dollars for the dinner, but you may get a million-dollar idea or contact out of it. The more financially savvy individuals I associated with, the more my financial wealth began to grow.

My dream was to associate with people who had global influence and global thinking and made global service contributions to humanity. I wanted to meet presidents, prime ministers, celebrities, and leading corporate CEOs, just to find out what they're doing and why and how they are doing it. I didn't necessarily want to be those people in all respects, but I wanted to empower my life socially and be able to play in the same global game instead of being at the bottom of the barrel of life, where I would be unable to self-actualize and would have to live by somebody else's values, rules, and objectives. I wanted to find out what it's like to be at the top of the mountain and dictate my destiny instead of having my destiny dictated to me. I'm now certain that that's doable. I'm watching it manifest in my life, because I'm following the principles that I am sharing, and they have worked. I have met and interacted with thousands of global players now.

I noticed in my own life that as long as I was devaluing myself, my influence was devalued and was growing

smaller. As I valued my time, myself, and my service, my
influence grew, and now I have the opportunity to share
my ideas with and influence millions of people yearly.

Now the more influence you have, the more accountabilities and responsibilities you have as well. Life doesn't
get easier. It's not about getting easier; it's about getting
more accountable and tackling ever greater challenges with
ever greater services.

It is wise and fruitful to surround yourself with people
that are inspired by what they do and have global influence, whether it be an artist, a poet, a writer, a politician, a
celebrated musician, artist, educator, or sports figure. One
idea from one contact may save you thirty years' worth of
learning and work. It's like a tennis pro. If a tennis pro
keeps playing with people that are not masterful, they
probably won't upgrade their performance. But what do
you think would happen to your tennis game if you played
with the top players?

I suggest that you make a list of people that have
expanded areas such as consciousness, spirituality, the
mind, business and finance, social networks, health,
beauty, fitness, and vitality and associate with them. If you
can help them achieve what they would love to achieve in
life, they'll be more likely to help you achieve what you
would love to achieve in life.

I keep an ongoing list of Nobel Prize winners. Every
time a great humanitarian achiever wins a Nobel Prize, I
get on the Internet, find out their information, and read
about their lives and unique work. In some cases, I have
called or contacted them. Sometimes I don't get a response,

but sometimes I do. Once I called two-time Nobel laureate Linus Pauling. He was one of my chemistry heroes when I was younger. Lo and behold, I got Linus Pauling on the phone. I talked to him for twenty minutes. His inspiring statements brought me to tears. He said, "I'm so invigorated to be able to do what I do. I can't wait to go into my laboratory tomorrow and see if I can make at least one more new discovery." At that time—1981—he was eighty years of age.

It is mind-blowing to realize that if some great achiever has accomplished an amazing feat that has inspired you, you have the power to do something equivalent. So I recommend this internal affirmation: "If Bill Gates, Warren Buffett, or Jeff Bezos can be a billionaire, so can I." They have two legs, two arms, a brain, a body. They get up and go to the bathroom in the morning, just like everybody else.

These are some of my internal dialogues or affirmations: "If so-and-so can be a multimillionaire or billionaire, so can I." "If somebody can have a global influence, so can I." "If somebody can change the paradigm of history, so can I." "If I am willing to do whatever it takes, travel whatever distance, and pay whatever price, to fulfill my primary service of love, or primary objective, it can be mine."

It's not just what you do; it's also how you perceive what you do. If you're constantly asking, "How is whatever is happening going to help me build financial wealth?" then no matter what happens, you'll be linking and building ideas to create your financial objective. That's the beauty and power of your inspired mind. The great American psy-

chologist and philosopher William James said the greatest discovery that human beings made in his generation
(around the turn of the twentieth century) was that they
could alter their lives by altering their perceptions and attitudes of mind.

Financial wealth building is partly a state of mind. The
individuals who have built vast fortunes have the same
bodies and life spans as you. But they built their financial
wealth or fortunes primarily because of their value structure. Their pursuit of what was highest on their list of values awakened in them their willingness attitudes, and their
perceptions, decisions, and spontaneously actions as well
as their display of discipline and focus. All of this led to
the relentless pursuit of their great mission of service and
reward.

The number one thing I've learned about financial
wealth building is the importance of transforming your
list of values and having financial wealth building become
higher on that list. As I've already said, the second you
appreciate it, you start having it come into your life.

If you had only twenty-four hours to live, could you
say that you did everything you could with everything you
were given? Did you use your mental and physical capacities to the fullest? Did you use your visual capacity, your
thinking capacity, your auditory capacity, your body, your
actions, your skills, your network of people to the fullest?
Did you use your money earning capacity, management,
and investment skills to the fullest? If you can say yes,
you've probably already lived an incredible and financially
fortunate life.

It's not unwise to associate with people that have vast visions and dreams and have accomplished amazing and inspiring achievements. If you do, it will rub off on you and assist you in serving more and helping you build greater financial wealth.

Share What You Learn

If you perceive a value in some of the ideas I am presenting here and if you truly want to learn this material, share it with somebody you love. By sharing or teaching it, you tend to learn, retain, and apply it more effectively. Probably no one walks their talk completely, but you can certainly increase your probability of doing so by helping other people do the same thing. I also learned these principles by helping other people learn them. There's no reason you can't do the same.

I also recommend reading the biographies of great and financially wealthy people. You'll find out that they've been through some or many of the same struggles and challenges as you. Then you'll realize if they can do it, so can you.

I did an exercise with my daughter. I knew some of the trials and tribulations she's been through. I looked through the biographies of famous people whose experience matched hers. I asked her—I paid her—to do book reports on their lives.

Afterwards I asked, "What did you learn?"

She said, "I realized that a lot of these famous or high-achieving people have been through the same trials and tribulations."

Why do you think I requested her to do that exercise? So she could realize that no matter what happens to her, she can use it to her advantage and build something great with her life. I was trying to offer her an investment that would last a lifetime. If I didn't pass such a torch on to her, she might pay a higher price for learning it later.

The Kleenex Holder

Once when I was practicing as a chiropractor in the early 1980s, I was hiring a business manager. A male candidate came into my office and said, "I'm the perfect guy for you." He was very zealous.

So I asked him a simple job screening question: "If I handed you a $10 million check right now and you didn't have to work for the rest of your life, what would you do?"

"I would do woodworking. I love making furniture."

"So that's what you'd love to do."

"Yes, absolutely."

A second later, I got up from sitting at my desk and escorted him out to the front door and thanked him for applying.

He asked me if he had been selected for the position.

I said no.

He asked me why.

I stated: "If you're such a great manager, why are you not doing professional woodworking? If you are not able to manage your life in a way that you can do what you truly love, love what you do, and get handsomely paid for it, why would I hire you to run my company, when you haven't yet managed to run your own life?"

He looked at me, totally humbled, and said, "I didn't know I was going to run into someone like you today, with a question that was so much to the point."

"Well, thank you for applying. May you consider becoming a woodworking professional. I believe this is where you will excel."

That was one question I asked during my screening process to find out what people are really dedicated to. I ask them, if I gave them $10 million, would they do that job? If not, I don't want to hire them. I would love to hire someone who would truly love and be inspired to do the job position I am offering.

This man said, "Dr. Demartini, that was a really eye-opening question. You're absolutely spot-on. I'm not the one for this job."

"Great," I said, "thank you for being honest."

He disappeared. Three weeks later, he came back into my office with a large brown paper bag and asked if he could meet with me once again.

When he came in, he said, "Dr. Demartini, I just wanted to say thank you."

"Why?"

"Because a few weeks ago, I came here and I was kind of cocky. I told you I wanted to take this position as manager. You asked me a humbling question. You made me realize that I wasn't really managing my own life. You made me stop and think about what I truly would love to do and why I wasn't living that life.

"I realized that I hadn't had a job for three months and I could go on for months like that, although my heart really wasn't into finding another job. My heart was really into making wood furniture. So, Dr. Demartini, I am in business. I got my first couch order the other day. It was a $1,200 couch. I know I'm going to build my business. I'm going to build a furniture manufacturing company."

"Fantastic," I said.

"I have a gift for you, Dr. Demartini, because what you said set me free for my life. When I was in your office, I noticed that in your exam rooms, you didn't have tissue holders. And I thought it would be nice to have tissue holders hanging on the wall that matched the woodwork in your office. I've custom-designed them, and I'd like to put them in your office."

"Absolutely."

He was very astute. Because his highest value was building furniture, he noticed the woodwork in my office. He's in business today doing what he loves to do and making more than I would probably have ever paid him.

There's always a way of doing the career action or service that inspires you, that you can't wait to get up in the morning to do, make a huge profit, and live in a kind of inspired state while doing that. The key is asking quality questions and taking high priority, quality actions.

3

The Nuts and Bolts of Wealth

A quality financial advisor can help you organize a master plan for your finances. They can take all of your accumulated assets, your goals, your dreams, your ambitions, your philanthropic objectives, your legacy, and where you want to be financially at different milestones, and help you structure a plan of action to accomplish these goals.

As you accumulate your financial wealth, it's also wise to have a certified accountant, a banker, periodic consultations with a tax attorney to avoid unnecessary taxation, and eventually an estate planner to establish and assure your legacy. You will want to become familiar with and come to know the evolving laws of your country of residence so thoroughly that you are not throwing away money unnecessarily.

There are different types of registered financial advisors and planners: they can range from overly optimistic risk-taking types to overly pessimistic risk-aversive types. They can also be product-driven and try to sell you financial products (often insurance policies) for which they receive an enduring trailer commission. There are also fee-for-service advisors, with no conflict of interest or product sales.

The more optimistic advisors can take your country's financial and taxation governing rules right to the edge, which can be complex and risky. The overly pessimistic ones can be more conservative and say, "No, don't take any risks. Just keep it simple and safe." They can sometimes be simpler and more cautious. They all may understand the mathematics but may not understand the state of mind game. It is wise to understand your hierarchy of values and make sure their final financial advice or plan of action is truly congruent with your highest values and objectives, your risk tolerance, your time horizons, and your philanthropic intentions.

The method of your financial planner's or advisor's payment is relevant also. As stated previously, advisors who are being paid by commission are, of course, going to be a bit optimistic about what they're selling you. Other financial managers are fee-for-service: you pay for their services by the hour, and they don't have any incentive to sell you financial products. They're usually more balanced. I recommend getting a balanced advisor, and that takes some questioning processes. I also think it's wise to seek out referrals and interview a number of advisors. No harm in doing that; you might pick up ideas and insights along the way. It's prudent to screen your potential financial advisors and get mentoring until you feel more certain. When the student is ready, the teacher appears. Sometimes it's time to go on to a new teacher or financial advisor and keep expanding instead of holding on out of loyalty. I eventually went beyond my first financial advisor's assumptions and level of expertise. There will be times when you grow into greater and more complex visions than the people that were once helping you. Allow yourself and your dynamic financial team to keep growing or evolving when required.

Nonetheless, it's valuable to have a trusted team of advisors, because an advisor will ask you some questions that will help you know yourself and your objectives. The more you know yourself and the more understanding you have about business and finance, the less you may require mentors. But along your journey, you're wise to step on the shoulders of giants in order to see greater possibilities and horizons.

Associating with Financial Wealth

Companies or corporations work on the same principle of association as individuals. Say you have a $10 million company. If you fill your CEO position or board with people that have $100 million companies, it will probably help your company grow to $100 million. Business leaders who already have achieved bigger visions, higher levels of complexity and operation, and greater financial outcomes will in all probability help your company go to that level. If you want to take your company from $1 million to $10 million or wherever the next level may be, you want to associate with and hire people on the next level and have them leading or guiding the way.

It is wise and productive to associate with people that have already demonstrated greater service and value. If you wouldn't be willing to pay for their advice, that's probably not someone to get advice from. If you're willing to pay for it, that means you feel that their advice will be valuable, and it could help you grow your business.

Some people will pay $10,000 or $100,000 for an hour with business titans, and they'll ask them one or two business questions that might turn a company around entirely. In this situation, you often get what you pay for. The more you pay, the more you will probably apply the advice you receive. That which circulates the most often has the least value. That which circulates the least often has the most value.

Three Levels of Wealth Building

There are three progressively riskier levels of building financial wealth: saving, investing, and speculating. My advice is to save before you invest and invest before you speculate (if you ever even want to speculate). It is wise to earn the right to handle greater levels of risk and reward. Excessive speculation is not essential for becoming financially wealthy. In other words, you are wise to crawl before you walk, and walk before you run.

I've had the opportunity to present many live seminars to some of the well-known financial investment companies like Merrill Lynch, Oppenheimer, Schwab, Fidelity, FNB,

Investec, and Westpac, and to many of their money managers, investment advisors, and brokers. The fact that they are financial specialists does not in itself mean that they are savvy managers of their own money. Many are placed in corresponding job positions, but many are also living beyond their means, and they may not have any significant accumulated net worth; they may actually have a negative net worth and debt. In a financial company for which I presented and consulted, only 4 percent of 200 advisors and brokers had a clear $2 million in net worth. That's eight people. And they were senior advisors to other advisors and hundreds of clients.

Some financial managers are living on the high end of lifestyles while being leveraged out to the hilt and having no substantial money saved or invested, or any significant net worth at all. The do not have financial wealth building among their top values and are often focused more on living a fancy lifestyle than on true wealth building. They are often impatient and want the fancy, immediately gratifying life now.

Because patient, methodical, financial wealth building is not high on their list of values, they often try to get rich quick through trading and speculating (possibly like some people you know, or even you). They may be putting you into speculative gambles that make them money by buying and selling with high turnovers, without providing you with any real stability or true intrinsic value.

Many speculative investments are structured, packaged, and marketed to make the customer feel they will receive the biggest yields in the shortest period of time. As a result, the customer can appear to have big, highly leveraged returns for a year or two and become foolishly, emotionally, and irrationally exuberant while the package is overpriced above the mean and then suffers big crashes for two or three years when the market corrects. If you're caught in this situation, you can become manic and extroverted, thinking you're successful during the up phase and getting depressed and wanting to sell out some or all of your profits on the down phase, so that you're back to where you were, or zero. If you are not able to govern your emotions don't expect to manage your money wisely. When your become irrational and manic, you will probably take foolish actions with your money and speculate on highly volatile trading instead of patiently and soundly investing.

Once a lady called my Houston office from Australia. She said, "I've got $28,000 saved. That's all of my entire nest egg. A friend of mine has told me that he can guarantee 15 to 20 percent return in one year if I lend him the money so he can invest it for me in a hot IPO" (initial public offering of stock).

"Do not give him anything," I said, "because, in my opinion, you're not in the league to play that game. You are not an eligible investor with $100,000 in total assets and are not ready for risky speculations such as an IPO. If he is offering this IPO to someone ineligible and asking for you to provide him with your entire savings, his qualifications and intentions are highly questionable. Even if you were to do it, don't give him more than 10 percent of your money, which is $2,800. If you can't get into the deal he wants for $2,800, walk away from the deal."

Here's why. No one with any financial savvy, account-ability, or respect would encourage a beginning saver and investor to speculate with their entire life's savings on such a risky position. Remember, it is wiser to save before you invest and before you speculate. An individual who is con-siderate and accountable would not gamble with other people's life savings and place them in such volatile and unpredictable speculations. It is wiser to first have a sub-stantial three- to six-month cash reserve or cushion in place and layers of sound investments on top of your savings before gambling with your hard-earned money. A respect-ful investment advisor or broker would not let you gamble on such speculations unless you can truly handle the vola-tility and potential gain or loss. Many of those speculations won't even let you in unless you have a net portfolio worth at least ten times their minimal amount and are an experi-enced and accredited investor. It would be foolish for this woman to put all her eggs in one speculative basket: she has a high probability of saying goodbye to some, if not all, of her money.

If the IPO went up drastically, she could associate it with quick money gains, experience a high, and increase her odds of further gambling, which often leads to even-tual losses. If the stock went down drastically, she could associate it with quick money losses, experience a low, and increase her odds of no longer wanting to participate in the market, which could discourage her from future sound investing.

It's smart to override or govern the immediate urge to break a patient, long-term investment strategy, instead sticking to methodical, probable, and predictable approaches in order to remove the more reactive emotions. You will end up with more financial wealth in the long run; if you want to take those risks later, you'll have earned the right to do so. Then you can put some proportion of your money into speculations. Even if they go up or down, you won't be distressed, because they account for less than 10 percent of your portfolio.

When I was about thirty-three, I was asked to be a guest on a financial radio show with Bill Woods in Houston, Texas. Bill Woods was a financial advisor who had been on the radio for decades. He had been around the block, and on the show he told me something a bit shocking. He said he had gone through over 10,000 clients in the years that he'd been in business and looked at their initial portfolios. He said the net average return for the average investor that was desperately trying to get rich quick had been averaging around 2 percent or less, primarily because of the front-end or back-end loads, management fees, trading fees, federal, state, or city short-term capital gains and dividend taxes, low returns, and speculation losses.

You may have made some impatient decisions and actions that have lost you money in the past. You may have gotten involved in an investment that went up; you were a bit blinded by the acceleration above the mean; then it may have crashed or corrected. You either sold it below the mean or had to ride the cycle out, and you were temporarily wounded.

When you become wounded and bleed a bit, sharks, Ponzi schemers, and con artists can emerge and seem to be saviors. When you feel you have been wounded by a loss, you can unconsciously send out a signal saying, "I'm hurting or bleeding," since you do not want to lose all your money and would love to get it back quickly. Sharks come in with get-rich-quick schemes to get the rest of your money while you're down. That is why risky speculation and volatile emotions can interfere with financial wealth building.

The most important thing to do is, first, save to build a stabilizing cushion, then patiently and wisely invest in sound investments with true intrinsic value before speculating. Recently I met a man who has $8 million in savings. He kept it in the least likely place: a bank. For all these years, he's put all his money in a bank, often making very little more than inflation. But he says, "I have never lost any money." If you never lost any money, would you still be farther ahead than you are today?

That is a bit extreme. Savings by itself will not accumulate enough financial wealth to override inflationary erosion and will not allow your money to compound sufficiently. The savings portion of your portfolio is primarily for your initial stable foundation, for emergencies, and for taking periodic advantage of exceptional true value investing. Your investments are for growth. There are progressive classes of investments that yield ever greater returns to help you accelerate the growth of your capital.

Benjamin Graham, known as the father of value investing, said the key is not to lose—to preserve your principal. Often people are trying to sell you on how to leverage yourself to make huge returns very quickly. During the upswing of the market, people are making fortunes, but they're very vulnerable during that time. When the market goes in the other direction, these people sometimes lose great fortunes or are stuck with great debts or margin calls. Overleveraging has its downsides.

This conservatively saving gentleman just kept his money secured. He methodically saved until he had accumulated $8 million and never lost any of his money, other than through erosion due to inflation. He was still more fortunate than a lot of people that try to make big killings quick, get depressed when the market goes down, then sell and go back to where they started. As Benjamin Graham said, time *in* the market is more significant than timing of the market. Time in the market is first savings and then patient, wise, compounding, intrinsically valued investments. Savings will not produce more than value investing, and sound investing will probably produce more than most speculation. In short, it's wise to build some savings before you invest or speculate. If you do, you've earned the right to risk.

Financial advisors commonly ask you verbal questions or use prewritten questionnaires to attempt to identify your risk tolerance. I believe that at times this procedure can be misleading. Nine times out of ten, if the market is in a bull phase, people exaggerate the risk levels they can handle. When it's a bear market, they're scared and risk-averse. If they are not governed and focused on the long-term and do not set realistic expectations according to the mean, these advisors can then overleverage with other people's money when the market is overpriced and up above the mean and sell out when the market is down and below the mean.

They foolishly become elated and buy at the top and freak out and sell at the bottom. You don't get a true reading of how you will truly react under volatile movements with a simple questionnaire.

A more accurate way to determine an individual's true risk tolerance level is to find out how their savings and investment portfolio is currently allocated. If they really have a sufficient cash cushion or reserve to handle the risk involved in volatile market swings, they will have a higher risk tolerance. The greater the cash reserve, the less probable it is that their ungoverned emotions will initiate foolish overreactions. Until you can manage your emotions, don't expect to manage your money. If somebody says, "I want you to take all your money and put it in this high-risk investment," and you don't have a cash savings cushion and a layer of sound investments underneath you, you really haven't earned the right to put all or even much of your money in that speculative basket.

But if you've got a cushion of cash, another cushion of bonds, and another of stock or real estate investments, and the portion you're speculating with is small—preferably no more than 10 percent of your total financial wealth—you can handle it. This has been demonstrated historically: people can handle 10 percent in fluctuations without overreacting. With any more than that, they're probably going to react foolishly, regardless of what they tell you.

After interviewing many people, I would say that most of them evaluated their own risk tolerance inaccurately. Their assumptions were exaggerated or minimized and emotionally based. When the market went up, they exaggerated its advantages; when the market went down, they minimized them. The key factor was their liquid assets. The more cash liquidity they had, the more tolerance they truly had. If they had a sufficient savings cushion, they were stable; if they didn't, they were unstable and over- or underestimated their actual risk tolerance level.

Let's explore how this can affect somebody. Say you earn $1,000 a day in your business and you have zero money in savings. If you have a $5,000 day, how are you going to feel? Emotionally elevated! Next, you have a $50 day. How do you feel? You go from elevated to emotionally depressed. If you have zero money, it's hard to override the emotions of volatility. You are extrinsically driven instead of intrinsically stable. But if you have $100,000 in liquid cash reserve, you're much less likely to overreact to an up or down day.

That's why companies that have large capitalization* and large cash reserves are more stable and less volatile than those with small capitalization and small cash reserves. The greater the capitalization and cash reserve, the greater the stability. Capitalization and cash reserves stabilize companies. You increase the quality of your clients thereby, because you're not eager to take on desperate ones. Capitalization, savings, and stabilization increase predictability and certainty in companies, whereas undercapitalization often kills them.

An important point to remember is capitalization. Say you have the choice of putting your money into further sta-

---

* Capitalization: market cap = current share price x outstanding shares.

bilizing your company with extra cash reserves and quality investments versus speculating to get a big immediate killing in a new startup gamble. Stabilizing your company is probably going to give you a greater long-term return than putting it into a speculative unknown with high volatility, even though the latter might get a bigger immediate return. The stabilization of your company is probably going to earn you a greater yield in the long term. To that you can add the advantages of the stabilization of your psyche and the development of self-discipline and patience. After all, your company is your primary source of income until your investment income eventually becomes greater and exceeds your primary income source. Anything you can do to stabilize your primary income is to your advantage.

Most people can tolerate about a 10 percent fluctuation in the market without foolish emotional reaction. Whenever you have more than ten times the average volatility in cushion, you stabilize your company. That's why the average individual in the world's industrialized nations has about a 10 percent debt level: they can only tolerate about a 10 percent in gain or loss without emotionally reacting. That's also why religions have asked for tithes of 10 percent: they knew people could tolerate 10 percent without reaction, but that's about the most they could do.

If you have $1 million invested and its value drops to $900,000 because the market goes down 10 percent, you won't like it, but you probably won't foolishly sell out; you'll just ride the wave. But if it drops 20 or 30 percent, you're more likely to foolishly sell at the bottom and guarantee a capital loss. If it goes up 20 to 30 percent, you're likely to go into a manic phase and foolishly overleverage. You'll tend to buy on margin, borrowing other people's money and taking other unwise actions.

That's why saving is wiser to start with than investing or speculating. It stabilizes your emotions and helps you maintain your strategic focus once you invest. And investing is wiser to do before speculating, because it's very helpful to earn the right to handle ever greater degrees of volatility and risk capacities.

Paying Yourself First

Let's recapitulate what we've found so far. To begin with, your hierarchy of values dictates your financial destiny. In order to build financial wealth, it's helpful to raise saving and then investing higher on your hierarchy of values. Liquidity is essential, and following strategies is wiser than impulses.

Furthermore, it's important to value yourself: if you don't value yourself and declare your worth, don't expect somebody else to. The wealthy pay themselves first, and they make sure they have built a stabilized foundation of financial cushions.

There are two factors in financial wealth building that are worth emphasizing: having a greater financial wealth building vision and having a greater financial cushion. The greater your vision—your cause—the more stable you are. If you have a vast vision to make millions of dollars and you make a $5,000 in one day, you're not likely to get manic about it: you'll just say, "Great; next step." The more stable you are emotionally, the more money you will probably make, because money flows to where there's greater certainty and flows away from those with emotional volatility or uncertainty.

As we've seen, the world values you to the degree that you value yourself. Moreover, your situation will shift radically if you pay yourself first. When you invest in you, so do others.

Let me illustrate this point with an example from my own case. When I first opened up my chiropractic practice, I was not fully aware of my true value. I did not know what value and contribution I could yet make to others or this world. I came into the office before everybody else and left after everybody else. I served patients for long hours. If any income was left over after all the office, personal bills, and taxes were paid, I lived off it.

I had an assistant, who started with me, and I then hired another within months. Then I kept adding assistants and doctors and kept growing my business. But I still didn't have much to show for it, because the more I grew my business, the more I kept putting money back into it by hiring more people. I didn't have much left over for myself. Months into the business, I was overbusy, doing lower-priority actions and burning out, because I still didn't have much profit. Everybody else was getting paid on time, and I was getting what was left over.

Then, at a pivotal point in time, a lady who had worked for me for six weeks suddenly gave her notice. She said she was getting married, she was moving, and she wouldn't be with us anymore.

"This lady's never missed a paycheck," I thought, "but she's not dedicated to the company. I'm the one that's in the office the most hours, and I'm taking whatever's left over. This whole thing is backwards."

At that point I learned a major principle about prioritization: you pay the founding owner, who is most vital and number one, next you pay the taxes, and then you pay your employees and expenses or bills in order of priority. Nobody but you is going to get up in the morning and do everything they can to help you become viable in business and wealthy.

So I changed my priorities. I decided I was going to pay people according to the priority of their value in the company, including myself. I thought, "Who and what is really most important in this company, and who's and what is second and third most important?" That was a turning point in my life—the beginning of my financial wealth growth. Wisdom is paying people and expenses according to priority. I electronically automated as many payments as possible to get any my emotions out of the way of building lasting wealth.

My top priority was whoever would penalize my business most if I didn't pay them. I realized that if I didn't reward myself and I burned myself out, that was going to cost my company more than anyone and anything. Similarly, it would penalize me heavily if I didn't pay my personal and company taxes. So I pay myself first, pay my taxes second, pay my lifestyle third, and pay my business bills fourth. (When I say I pay myself first, I'm referring to what I call my immortality savings and investment account: money, capital, or assets I don't touch for many years or for the rest of my life.)

I started this approach the month that lady left, and that was the beginning of my wealth building. Until then, I kept breaking even and no better. It was at the time the financial planner appeared in my office. Out of ignorance, most businesspeople pay their business bills first, pay a little bit of their lifestyle, get behind on their taxes, and have little or no savings or investments.

I suggest that you say this affirmation right now: *I pay myself first because I'm worth it. I'm currently the most valuable and important one in my company. I'm vitally important in my household because I make my household's financial stability possible.*

Now I'd like you to write down how much you feel you could begin saving today. I don't want you to either exaggerate it or minimize it. I just want you to figure out a number that makes you say, "I know I can do that per week, per two weeks, or per month." How much could you save right now? I don't care how small it is, but I suggest that you write that figure down. It is not how much you save; it is the habit of saving that counts most. I started my savings with only $200 a month and then kept raising it from there and then began investing methodically. There is no risk in saving, since you have the money sat aside to pay any bills. Once you begin to save and then invest, your unexpected bills begin to decline in order to reward you. If you don't bring order to your financial house, disorder will emerge. Unexpected bills are signs of disorder.

Now add 10 percent to that figure. If it's $100, make it $110. If it's $1,000, make it $1,100. If it's $10,000, make it $11,000. You want to start saving in the zone between comfort and discomfort. If you're comfortable at one figure and you can tolerate an additional 10 percent without reaction, that is a good place to start. If you are the owner of your business, you can total up its gross income and allocate a percentage or a minimum amount (whichever is greater) for your business and individual savings cushions and investments. Never go below the fixed committed amount, only above.

Congruent Goals

Another important feature of your financial wealth building strategy is to make sure you have congruent goals. A doctor might say, "I want to have a million-dollar practice." OK, how many patients do you want to see? And how much will you earn per patient? How many hours do you want to work? They tell me; I calculate and find that their goals are contradictory and incongruent. The number of visits you project will lead you to a $700,000 practice, not a million-dollar practice. You have incongruent goals. What happens when you put in incongruent information into a computer? It deletes it. The same thing occurs in the brain: it deletes incongruent information or financial objectives.

It's wise to have dreams and goals that are congruent, not only aligned with your own highest values but with any others involved. One doctor said, "I want to see this volume of patients. I want to play golf three times a week.

I want to take this many trips." I calculated and found that that amounted to 420 days out of the year. It's like having a business plan that doesn't make sense.

Once in a while, *Forbes* magazine publicizes the assets of very wealthy people. I look at the ratios of their assets, and I found that many if not most of them are very conservative. Most of these superrich people are not huge risk-taking gamblers, except occasionally and only to a highly calculated extent. They study the odds and probabilities of returns on their investments and maintain adequate liquidity for unexpected outcomes or emergencies. They might dedicate a small percent of their portfolios to riskier investments, even though that amounts to millions of dollars. Then the media show hosts say that this individual is putting $50 million into this risky venture, but that is a tiny fraction of the portfolio of a multibillionaire. People hear about it and think, "I should do that," so they stick all of their wealth into that investment. For all we know, that investor may be using it as a write-off in the first place.

We often get false, misleading, or partial information from the media sources and pundits. That's why they are not necessarily your greatest financial advisors. In many cases what they say sells more than it serves. In most cases their opinions fluctuate from week to week or month to month. If you read the newspapers, you're going to see doomsday one week, recovery the following week, boom the next week, and doomsday again the following week. It's extremely unwise to let yourself be run by those transient and highly polarized pronouncements. They lead to emotional responses, and emotions are transient; long-term strategies, visions, inspirations, and what you love are more stable, lasting, or eternal. It is wise to focus on the latter. Don't let the wavering, wandering emotions interfere with your mission of service and your objective of rewarding financial wealth building.

Saving for Business

Here are two ways I recommend going about saving and investing for you individually and for your business: a minimal amount per month or a percentage, whatever's greater. I have a minimal amount guaranteed regardless of what my company does. When I have an extra big month, I take the extra money and add or transfer it into savings and then stairstep a portion of that automatically and electronically into quality investments. If you do only a percentage, you're going to have some degree of volatility based on whether your company goes up and down.

Now watch this. If you save and then invest a minimum amount, your company won't go below a certain amount, because you're making a declaration and an automatic, electronic commitment: "I'm worth this amount. My company's worth this amount; this is what is going to happen." Since I've started doing a minimum amount, I've not missed it. It stabilizes your business income. This highly organized demand impacts your supply. When I receive a bigger amount, I just put extra away; I add even more to my savings and investments. Some months I may have nothing extra, But somehow I just receive enough to transfer the minimum amount. Some months I may have an extra $60,000, and I'll put that extra away. I have done this for more than four decades.

I do the same thing with taxes. A predetermined portion of my income goes to taxes, and the rest goes into the savings and investments that I have collectively called my immortality accounts. My goal was to get to a point where my money in my immortality account at an annual 8 percent was earning me more than working, so I didn't have to work. But I continue working, because I love to share my work.

Self-Worth and Productivity

Your self-worth has a lot to do with your sense of productivity. People that stop doing some sort of service that makes a difference in others lives tend to erode their sense of value. That's why some older people constantly contact their kids: "Anything I can do for you?" They don't feel quite worthy unless they're doing some meaningful service for somebody. We're designed to serve our fellow humans and have a cause greater than ourselves, and we are rewarded with grateful feelings of fulfillment. We have a motor cortex in our brain for service and a sensory cortex for reward. When these are equitably balanced and we have created a sustainable fair exchange with others, we feel gratefully fulfilled.

As your savings grow, they're going to build a reserve or cushion. As they build a cushion, it's going to stabilize your emotions. If you own a company, a cushion is going to stabilize your company. A cushion enables you to increase the quality of your clients. If you've got $1 million saved as a cushion and a client comes in and doesn't match what you would love to have as an ideal client or customer, you can say, "I'd love to serve you, but I have someone more suitable I'd love to refer you to." You can be choosy about whom you want to serve. You will not be desperate, living from day to day. The greater your cushion, the higher quality customer you can have.

Again, occasionally you will be approached by people that you might prefer not to do business with. If you've got zero in your savings cushion, you may feel like you have to take them on as a client or customer, because you're desperate. If you have plenty of money in savings and investments, you don't have to take that client on; you can refer them out to somebody else that matches their needs more congruently. Consequently, having a savings cushion or liquidity enables the quality of your clients, the quality of your standards, and the quality of your service to go up. That can provide more lasting value than money in a high-risk investment or speculation, even if the latter has a higher yield.

Saving for Your Employees

Now if you have employees, this might be revealing to you: I recommend that your employees save and learn to invest also. In my company, I have been like the Big Brother that partly controls that. If you are up for a raise, I don't necessarily give you a full raise; I only give part of it to live on; the rest of it goes to savings and investments. I prefer not to give employees any less or more than 50 percent of their raise, because if I raise their lifestyle without raising their savings and investments, they're stressed, and they're again in desperation in a short period of time. But if I raise both their savings and their lifestyle, production and consumption maintain equilibrium. As for me, the late financial guru Sir John Templeton recommended saving and investing 50 percent of your income, so for many years I've done that. Whatever I get, 50 percent goes to savings and then investments. I pay taxes, bills and personal expenses on the rest.

Some individuals do not believe that is possible. I thought that initially too. But the greater the percentage I saved and invested, the more active and passive money I began receiving. And instead of raising my lifestyle, I just kept raising my savings and investments until the passive income exceeded my active income.

The more I invested in U.S. index fund stocks, the less taxes were due because of the low turnover rate and lower management costs. Furthermore, the long-term capital gains taxes are only 20 percent, dividends are reinvested or nonexistent, and taxation is deferred to the point of selling the shares.

I advise you not to overraise your lifestyle unless you raise your savings and then investments and taxes in equal amounts. This governs your lifestyle and makes sure you keep moving toward your goal of financial wealth building and freedom. Once your passive income approaches or exceeds your active income, you have earned the right to advance your lifestyle a bit. Buffett and Munger found it foolish to overdo their lifestyles. They kept their lives simpler. Vanity and luxury can trap and run you more than you may care to admit.

4

The Value of Taxes

Years ago, in my late twenties, I didn't like to pay taxes, because I was behind on them, and I would blame or devalue the government. Have you ever done that? You're behind on taxes, and you're angry at the government for making sure you have roads, city lights, sewage, water, and other services.

But just go live in a country that has a screwed-up tax system and little to no governed money management. People in such countries can't even rely on sewer, water, electricity, or telephones. Utilities don't work consistently. The banking system sometimes falls apart, and corruption often abounds.

If you have some experience in a country like that, you'll realize that paying taxes allows you to drive on streets with functioning streetlights and without potholes. It allows you to have running water, sewage, and all the other services we take for granted. You're not paying something for nothing; you're getting infrastructure, Social Security, health care, education, and defense.

You don't want to minimize government's contribution to your life. You may feel that a portion of your tax money is misappropriated. That is understandable, and you may even want to avoid paying unnecessary taxes, but it is unwise to evade taxes in a country that has taxation. By not appreciating taxes, you can make it even more challenging to pay them. It become more challenging to pay for what you are ungrateful for.

Of course, using every legitimate tax reducing, tax avoiding, or tax deferring strategy allowed within the country you reside in is a wise way to avoid paying unnecessary taxes and maximize your wealth.

I've spoken in over 150 different countries. Every one has different structures, some more socialized and democratic, some more individualized and autocratic. When I once presented a two-day financial wealth building program in France, people complained about income tax, Social Security, and other taxes. When you added all of them together, they had an 82+ percent tax rate, and they were basically living on 10 to 20 percent of their income. But they had cultural, social, and other health care services that some other countries didn't have. If they wanted that lifestyle and those social benefits, they were required to pay the price.

French society has a different value system from America's. They appear to love eating and socializing. Once a group of French health professionals asked me to do a seminar program on efficiency in Paris. I was scheduled to start presenting at eight o'clock in the morning. Around 9:45, the doctors attending started trickling in. We suddenly had tea and coffee presented for nearly forty-five minutes, and then we started to get back together. We had about sixty minutes of presentation; then they had lunch, and that was a two and a half hour experience. And they wanted to do a seminar on efficiency!

It was very frustrating at first until I realized that the topic they requested me to present was not what they were truly pursuing. Their idea of efficiency revolved more around social engagement than business productivity. I adjusted my expectations and over the years I gradually introduced some additional principles that shifted the participants' values and ideas of efficiency, particularly in regard to business and life in general. This catalyzed economic return to them, and productivity gradually became elevated on their list of values.

The French collective value system dictates the destiny of that country. In fact, every country's collective value system determines its fate. As the collective hierarchy of values change, so does the country. If it places a high value on saving and investing, it becomes more financially stable. If instead it places a high value on consuming, it becomes a volatile country. Then there is tension between the few haves and the many have-nots, and the nation eventually becomes economically unstable.

I strongly advise appreciating the opportunity to be paying your truly essential taxes. I don't think about paying my taxes anymore, because it's taken care of automatically and weekly. My accountant and financial manager are responsible for calculating my taxes and keeping them current and paid weekly, depending upon whatever I gross. If my income goes up for the month, they know to raise my estimated tax payments. It's automatically regulated. I don't want to have to think about it; I want it structured so that I can do what I am greatest at and love most—teach, research, write, travel, and inspire.

Of course, if you chose to live in a tax-free haven where there are no or minimal income taxes, that is a viable choice too. But other restrictions or challenges will come with it, like high living costs or low infrastructure standards.

Money That's Not Yours

You may have been surprised earlier to see that I put taxes as my second priority (after paying myself). Why? It's not wise to attempt to build your wealth on money that's not yours. It is wise to set that money aside and earn interest on it while it's in storage before it goes back to the government.

You're not likely to get by without paying any taxes unless you have structured your business to defer or offset taxes to later periods or have passed them on to a registered charity. Offsetting taxes with ever expanding and overleveraged debts has its downsides. There are legitimate ways to reduce your taxes, but it's not feasible to avoid them entirely without careful legal business and estate structuring. I know some people who have tried; they got away with it even for eight or ten years. But they ended up paying. The laws and rules are evolving to increase the probability that at least some amount of taxes is paid.

I'm financially wealthy, and I still pay my optimum portion of taxes, so you can do both. You're not going to miss any money by paying your share. You can still become financially free even with paying your optimized portion of taxes.

There is an additional value in paying your optimized portion of taxes. Whenever you contribute to something that you participate in and is at a higher level of social order and organization than you, you are contributing to, and in a sense investing in, something greater than yourself. It helps integrate and bring more order to society and contributes to a higher-quality social environment. Even though many politicians blow or possibly misappropriate some of the tax money, they don't blow all of it. Some of it is actually being used wisely and for essential causes that make the society work.

If you have issues about paying taxes, I advise you to write down 200 reasons why it is to your advantage to pay your portion of optimized tax. Why? Because it's harder to earn or come up with the money for paying your share of taxes when you consciously or unconsciously don't want to.

It's like what happens in divorce. When one ex-spouse is paying the other alimony, if the payers resents the other spouse and is angry and bitter, they have a higher probability of not earning the money to pay or simply not paying. But if they have a mutual arrangement and they're still working for the sake of the children, alimony is more easily paid.

You have difficulty paying for anything you devalue. If you devalue taxes, you have difficulty paying them. So if you're going to pay them, you might as well appreciate the value and purpose for them. Otherwise you're just making it harder on yourself.

Once you break the barrier of raging because taxes are evil and appreciate that they're just part of social life, you don't mind setting money aside for them. Once I set the tax money aside, I don't even consider it mine; I just see it as paying another bill.

I put aside about 2 percent more than my estimated taxes, so I do not have unexpected quarterly surprises. I accumulate money in my tax account; that's now additional savings. I'm earning a small amount of interest on the money that I will pay the government or tax authorities. I'm only making 4 or 5 percent from it, but to me, that's sufficient to keep up with inflation.

Some people say, "I'm not going to pay taxes until the last minute. I'm going to put the money into a risky investment. I'll make three times the amount of money I need to pay. I'll sell it when I need to, and I'll pay my taxes." But they can't always sell their investment when they need to. This initiates further short-term capital gains taxes; then they sometimes have to borrow money to pay the taxes off. It becomes an entanglement instead of a simple automatic weekly strategy.

My experience is that the more money you save and then invest, the less you'll end up paying proportionately in taxes. You'll actually pay more money, but less of a percentage as your investments compound. And it's valuable to remember that the more you pay in taxes, the more you've earned, and the more you're contributing to society. It is wise to optimize your tax deductions and advantages, but pay what is due.

You pay the most taxes when you work for others. You pay less taxes when you work for yourself and have deductions. You pay the least taxes once you have invested and can defer taxes through long-term capital gains.

5

Savings and Investments

The masses live in the illusion of gain and loss. The master knows there's no ultimate gain or loss; there's only transformation. Constant transformation, not gain or loss. Freedom to come and go.

Wise financial management and long-term commitment to financial wealth building can free you from the perception of the gain and loss game. If you manage your money wisely, with sufficient savings cushions or reserves, you can get beyond the emotional reactions associated with the perceptions of gain and loss. You then just live in a world of transformation and financial fulfillment. But the journey begins once you start saving and then investing your money and accumulating ever greater sums of capital and assets.

When you have saved and invested $1,000, you can handle $100 fluctuations in the market with little emotional reaction and be patient during such transient market fluctuations.

When you have saved and invested $10,000, you can handle $1,000 fluctuations in the market with little emotional reaction and be patient during such transient market fluctuations.

When you have saved and then invested $100,000, you can handle $10,000 fluctuations in the market with little emotional reaction and be patient during such transient market fluctuations.

And so on. The more you save and invest, the longer your time horizons will probably become, and the less emotionally reactive you will become.

Long-term vision and patience can make you additional money. Immediate gratification can cost you money. Immediate gratification is saying, "I want this now," like a baby. Babies are spontaneous gratifiers. They look over their shoulder and scream to see if they'll get what they want. If they don't, they'll scream again. But if you talk to a ninety-year-old woman, she will probably tell you that patience is a virtue.

That's why it's important to know what you're going to do with your accumulated millions in the long term and know exactly how you're going to manage or allocate them: that demonstrates that you already know this to be true; you already have it in your consciousness; it's in your being.

You're Already Worth It

Another little exercise: to make a list of where you're currently worth that total amount of money already. That way, you already know you have its equivalent, and all you're going to do is transform it through a shift in your hierarchy of values. You don't ever truly gain or lose it. You just change its current form into financial assets or liquid cash. You're going to transform some of your other forms of genuine wealth and convert them into financial assets or liquid cash.

A lady in Sydney came to one of my seminar programs on self-mastery and leadership, and she wrote down one of her primary objectives and dreams. She wanted to be a leading corporate consultant, consulting for the top Fortune 100 Australian corporations. She was somewhat intimidated by the achievements of the CEOs of these corporations. I told her to write down twenty-five of the most liked and disliked behaviors she perceived that each of them displayed or demonstrated. Then she was to look within herself and her life, find each of these behaviors, and own every one of them quantitatively and qualitatively, whether they were in the same or similar forms, according to her own hierarchy of values. That way, she could see where she displayed and demonstrated everything that these CEOs had. She would no longer devalue herself and minimize her position relative to them and would begin to value herself and her contribution equally.

First she said, "But I don't perceive that I have all those admired behaviors or the same net worth."

"As long as you believe that," I replied, "you will lessen your probability of doing consulting for these individual leaders. So I want you to sit down and write down where you have displayed or demonstrated the same equivalent behavior until it is quantitatively and qualitatively equal to whatever degree you perceive in them. What form is it in? When you draw out unconscious information of your memory bank and make it conscious, you realize that the equivalent behavior is not missing in you. It is simply in a form you have not recognized, acknowledged, and honored."

When you are too humble to admit that whatever you perceive and admire in others lies within you, you will self-depreciate and play on a smaller playing field of opportunity. When you devalue yourself, so does the world. Once you own the traits of the greats, you give yourself permission to elevate the field so that you get to play in greatness.

This lady took one of the top CEOS in Australia and wrote down twenty-five of the most admired and disliked behaviors she perceived he displayed or demonstrated. She looked into her memory banks and made herself conscious of where and when she equally displayed or demonstrated the same behaviors until the quantity and quality matched.

This process took months of introspection to complete. As she was doing this exercise, her self-worth was going up, because she realized she had much more talent and hidden assets than she initially realized. Within three years, she became the consultant for this leading CEO and was being paid substantially more. It all started when she realized that whatever she perceived in that individual was already being displayed or demonstrated within herself. If she saw greatness, she had it inside herself. If she saw wealth, she had its equivalent degree of wealth inside herself, though it may be stored in other various forms. If she hadn't yet seen the equivalent forms it's in, she was accountable to look again and again until she discovered that nothing is missing within her.

Once you see that you have the equivalent worth of value or assets, you can transform its various forms into financial wealth by shifting your values and by raising financial wealth building up on the list of priorities. But until you can see the equivalent in your own mind, it's hard to convert it, because you don't feel worthy. Your perceived lack of self-worth holds you back. It's a game of the mind. Your equivalent wealth may be sitting in a dispersed set of forms involving your assets in social contacts, physical beauty, intellectual property, business leadership, financial investments, family connections, or spiritual awareness.

The world reveals and provides you with what you claim and already know you own. When you go to the bank for a loan, it's wise to realize you already have the equivalent amount in some genuine form of collateral wealth. Don't go in for a business loan without already knowing that you have its equivalent as collateral. Some of it may be in the form of your incredible business plan, your noted and respected management team, your intellectual property patents, your celebrated media status, or many other guises.

Planned Automatic Savings

Here's what I can encourage you to consider. You have already started your forced, automated, electronically transferred, saving deposits and are having your preselected amount deposited monthly, biweekly, or weekly into an interest-bearing, financial institution money market account. The amount is a progressively accelerated percentage of your income, preferably starting at least with 10 percent or a fixed minimum amount, whatever's greater. This is guaranteed: you are committed to save at least that amount per month or more frequently. There is no turning back, only forward and up.

I then run a projection on my calculator every quarter. If I save that amount every single month, using an estimated average compound interest, where will I be X years from now? I suggest that you do a chart of where you'll be one, five, ten, twenty, forty, fifty years from now—until the point where you think you're going to no longer earn income or die. You might as well plan to live to 100, because it's quite possible that you will. If you die at ninety, at least there will be some money left over.

Let's say you're saving $100, $1,000, or $10,000, or whatever amount, per month. Where will you be at the end of the year? Multiply your monthly savings rate by 12 plus the interest, accruing at, say, 8 percent. At five years, that's 60 months plus the interest. Run the numbers to your life expectancy. If you just committed to saving that amount, where would you be? It will give you an incentive to continue, and you will see the greater possibility of what you could save and then invest. In three months, increase your savings by 1–10 percent, run another projection every time you raise the amount, and keep updating your projections of where you're going to be quarterly.

Once you accumulate savings of at least 3-6 months of your company's gross income worth of cash reserves or a decent liquid savings cushion, it is time to begin investing. Or you can save and invest simultaneously along the way from the beginning. But it is important to build a savings cushion to stabilize your emotions and primary income source, so you do not become distracted by get-rich-quick impulses or gimmicks promoted by unscrupulous individuals.

As soon as your passive income from your saving, investments, compound interest, and/or dividends is equal to your active income—that is, from your primary source of earnings—you've achieved the first level of financial freedom or independence. Then you can say, "If I increase my savings and investments every quarter, I can become financially independent sooner and multiple times over."

I've seen people become financially independent from the advice I'm giving here faster than they imagined possible. The key is the consistency of the acceleration, or the increased quarterly amount saved and then invested. The quickest I've seen this achieved is two years; about the longest I've seen is beyond ten years, for those who have been less aggressive. I've seen an average of eight to ten years before people reach financial independence if they do what I'm about to recommend.

In under a decade, people can reach the point where their money is passively making them as much as they make by actively working. You want to keep those projected numbers in your wealth building file on your computer. I run projections and update all my finances on a quarterly basis, or whenever there has been substantial market gains.

I look at where I am now: my current net worth. Then I look at how much is going in per week, biweekly, or per month on average, and I run that projection at 8 percent. As you keep doing this, the amount you will put into savings and investments goes up, along with the compounding interest.

In a year or two, you'll be inspired to go further even faster. Compound interest is your greatest helper. The man who just did automatic savings and kept it all in the bank didn't earn a lot of interest on it, but he kept saving. It took him about eighteen years to start doubling his money. But now he's up to $8 million. It's not that the average individual doesn't make money; it's that they spend most of it. They don't save or invest much of their money.

If you are like most people, you've blown at least 10 percent of all the money that you've ever initially saved or invested. Maybe you got into some risky speculation, lost out, and had to start all over. If you had just kept saving and wisely investing it, you'd probably be in the same place without as many financial setbacks and stress.

Let's say you own a business. If you have at least three to six months of liquid capital to cover it, even if chaos ensues, that would give you enough time to figure out how to readjust your situation. The only time you're going to touch that reserve is if there's an emergency of epic proportions; otherwise you don't. You just let it keep growing and use it to stabilize your emotions and wisely follow your business and financial strategies. As that cushion keeps getting bigger, it will help your business keep getting bigger as well. Where money goes, money flows.

Bonds: The Next Step

As soon as you have at least a ninety-day cushion in a money market equivalent, if the interest rates are sufficiently high enough, you can put additional money into government bonds. They will not give you a big yield, but they will give you a bigger cushion for stability that exceeds the rate of inflation. It is wise to have enough of a cushion so that you never miss a night's sleep over concerns of cash flow.

I was doing consulting for a lady in New York whose net worth was hundreds of millions of dollars: 10 percent of her money was sitting in tax-free municipal bonds with fixed returns when the interest rates were higher. Another 10 percent was in highly rated corporate bonds. She had 20 percent in cash money market reserves and another 50 percent in stocks including her own company. The last 10 percent was a mixture of homes, art, and other collectibles. She was conservative and stable.

I believe it to be wise to build a stable financial base as a foundation for your portfolio and to be patient and methodical in your approach to become financially free.

I also recommend continually educating yourself and committing to mastering your financial or money management with foresight more than speculating and learning from hindsight.

There are certain basics that you can rely on: Money markets are more stable than bonds. Bonds are more stable than stocks. You're wise to only take additional risk when you've earned the right to that level of risk. Build layers of cushions with progressively higher yielding (although more fluctuating) investments. With very reliable savings and investments, the only risk is inflation eating away at your returns. But if you look carefully, you'll see that if there's inflation, money markets will go up too. Even though taxes and inflation may be eroding some of your earnings, you're still coming out a little ahead. You're generally wiser to be a little ahead with stability than apparently way ahead with instability and emotional vulnerability. But as you add layers of stabilizing cushions and go from money markets to bonds to stocks to higher yielding but more volatile stocks or to real estate investments, study the probabilities of risk and reward. Be a wise investor rather than an foolish and impulsive gambler.

So at first, you build your cash savings or reserves in the form of money market funds, then government bonds and corporate bonds. Anywhere you have no significant volatility and preserved principal, it's called *savings*. So those two classes—bonds and money markets—are called *savings*. Once you buy shares in quality, regulated, well-governed companies floated on the stock market or their collective indices or buy quality real estate holdings, it's called *investing*.

Buying Individual or a Group of Stocks

The third step is to buy individual stocks or their collective indices. I would discourage you from doing this until you have enough of a money market savings cushion that the amount you put into those stocks is moderated enough to keep you from overly elated or depressed when they temporarily go up and down, as they will continue to appreciate and rise long-term.

The more you concentrate your investment monies into a single stock or asset class, the higher the probability of volatility and of gaining or losing money; you're temporarily appearing to make or lose money. If it is a well-managed, quality stock and you hold it over the long term, it can become a very worthy asset. If the stock goes far up, you can appear to temporarily make a lot of money, but since each asset class generally has a mean average growth rate, if it exceeds this rate of growth, it will probably calm back down and return to or approach the mean over time. That's why at least some degree of diversification is not unwise. If you diversify, you may have a more moderated return, but you also have a more predictable future picture. Your portfolio doesn't rise or go down as fast, and you can set your mind at ease and be patient for a respectable return over the long term without emotional volatility extremes.

I discourage buying one individual so-called magical stock without any diversification: you may buy what everybody else is buying, which may be already too late, when it is overpriced, and you may unwisely sell after everybody else has sold, which is too early and underpriced. You're not as likely to make money by doing that. Sometimes trying to time the market is less fruitful than time in a quality market.

But if you do decide to invest in an individual stock, there are certain things you may want to do, such as make sure that that stock has more capitalization than debt. Why would you want to invest in a company whose executives may not manage its money wisely? I don't advise putting all of your investment money into a single stock when you don't need to.

A friend may have told you that this is the hottest new stock because it's been going up quickly for the last two months, but then you're maybe not really buying a quality stock; you may be buying a cultural and emotional contagion, which may have no substance or true intrinsic value. It is wiser to look at the fundamentals of the company and make sure it is truly one with value. Buying a hot new company when there is extreme emotional exuberance can turn out to be an illusion, because emotions are often ultimately illusions. When price/earnings ratios are excessive, beware.

If you are overly excited, your blindness to the downsides and risks will probably distract you from investing in quality, well managed investments. When you are a bit more sober, you are probably on track.

In the long run, it is wiser to buy true, intrinsically valued stock of quality companies that have track records of sustainable fair exchange and consistently and repeatedly purchased brand-name consumables. If the price of that stock is far over the earnings, value, and assets of that company, you're buying people's interpretation of that company rather than the fundamentals of the company itself. That can and will usually bite you. If you're going to buy a stock, it's wise to make sure that its assets and value are real and the price/earnings ratio is small enough that you're getting value out of that stock.

If you're going to buy a single stock, unless the stock is a solid company and the general market in its sector is temporarily and significantly down, I would not advise simply putting in one lump sum and saying, "All right, I'm going to do it and ride it up." My advice is, if you're going to buy a quality stock, consider buying it on a dollar-cost average basis. Instead of buying stock shares at a single price, with dollar-cost averaging you buy in smaller amounts at regular intervals, regardless of the fluctuating price. As a result, it doesn't matter as much whether the stock temporarily goes up or down. When it goes up, you make money on the past. When it goes down, you make money on the future. Either way, you make money over the long term if it is a quality stock and you keep buying it. Becoming a net long-term buyer can pay off. Like Warren Buffett, you hold a quality stock for the long haul, whether it goes up or down. If it's a well-managed, quality stock, it will go up in the long run.

You can also do value averaging. Here you are adjusting how much you put into the market each month based on your specific goals and how your portfolio is performing. Every month you select what dollar value you want added to that stock. If the stock goes up in value, you put less in. If the stock goes down, you put more in. You allow the capitalization based on the number of shares to match a certain figure each month. According to the mathematics, that gives you a 0.6 percent increase in return. Of course, this requires a bit of active managing instead of passively automating the deposit with a fixed, committed, but quarterly accelerated amount.

If you've accumulated millions of dollars in that stock, that's significant. If you don't, it's not probably worth the time and effort, because you have to time your purchases and actively participate, which can make you vulnerable to emotional reactions. It's simpler and probably wiser to just do dollar-cost averaging: you have a fixed amount going in. You don't need to think about it, since it is automated, and you can get on with your primary income generating career without distraction.

It's also advisable to know about the CEO of that company as well as what's going on in it. Otherwise, if there are shenanigans, you might find that you have thrown away your money.

That's why I recommend a bit of diversification—across sectors, across classes. You have a more predictable, though moderated, number as far as yield is concerned, regardless of volatility. You don't have to concern yourself about whether those stocks go up and down. You keep dollar-cost averaging.

The more stable stocks to invest in are generally large-cap blue-chip or name-brand stocks. Some examples: Coca-Cola, Apple, Microsoft, Pfizer, and Disney. Next are large-cap stocks: those with a market capitalization of over $10 billion. (Remember, I said that companies with large capitalization are generally more stable.)

These types of highly capitalized stock investments are an asset class that generally have long-term track records and name recognition. An asset class is a classification of assets with similar financial characteristics and with behave similarly in the marketplace. Each class teaches you something new about your risk tolerance as you invest in it.

So you're going to learn something in each new asset class you invest in. You are in a financial educational institution called life, and you go from class to class to class, earning the right to greater levels of risk the higher your go.

After large-cap stocks, you can go up the class ladder to mid-cap stocks, to small-cap stocks, to microcap stocks, to penny stocks. At this point, you transition from investment to speculation, because these smaller and often newer stocks have very little track record. You don't know what they're going to do in the long term. They don't have much capitalization, or history. You may receive a higher possible return, but you also have a higher volatility and potential loss. Once you transition up into speculations, you could also go into independent public offerings (IPOs)—stocks that have just gone on the market. They might give you a huge yield, or they might lose all the money you put in them.

I once presented a seminar program in Sydney, Australia, called "The Secrets to Financial Mastery," where I shared my Force Accelerated Savings Technique (FAST) and my Forced Accelerated Investment Technique. Seven gentlemen in that class of about fifty were multimillionaires who had lost their fortunes and had to go back down or to zero; some were in debt. They'd taken some savings and put some of it into overpriced real estate and some into overpriced stocks. The market went up. They said, "I'm making piles of money here, at least on paper." They started to use other people's money—OPM—and bought shares on margin or properties on loan and were overleveraged while the market was above the mean. The market was still initially rising and accelerating, so they were seemingly making more money on paper, and they were starting to believe they were invincible and blinded themselves. Pride before the fall.

One gentleman said he was up to $11 million on paper, and then all of a sudden, the stock market and real estate market nosedived and corrected. What he thought he had gained over the previous four years turned out to be smoke and air. The share and property price had no true foundational substance: now he had this property but didn't have a stable renter or a buyer, yet he still had to pay the taxes and other costs on it while also temporarily losing leverageable equity. He was highly leveraged out already with an unregulated and ungoverned bank. All the other people whose money these banks and investors had been using were suddenly demanding their money back, so the bank was forced to call its loans. He had little to no savings cushion; he was highly leveraged out. He ended up auctioning and fire-selling the property to pay the costs at a loss, and he lost all the gains he thought he achieved.

Varieties of Speculation

It is not wise to speculate before you invest or to invest before you save. But let's say you want to get more sophisticated, and you've got at least a year or two's worth of saved liquid capital. Now you'd like to have a little bit of so-called fun. You feel secure, and you want to speculate a little; you'd just like to see if you can play with your crystal ball in the market. Just know that you're now in competition with the greatest minds in this business, and few even of them will beat passive index funds over time.

Few money managers have consistently beaten the index funds.

If you decide to speculate, you're possibly going to hear terms like *IPOs, venture capital, futures, options, warrants,* and *derivatives*. Here you're buying on the fluctuations in the market. You're buying (or selling) an option to buy or sell a stock at a certain price at a certain date. You're gambling on foretelling the future of whether that stock is going to go up or down. Since nobody knows what the market's going to do, it's a gamble. Just know that it's a gamble, and the probability is mathematically not always in your favor in the long run.

In case you try to play with options, which I don't recommend for most people, except maybe with a small portion of your monies—maybe 1 percent of your portfolio—I recommend that you actually do that on paper for at least three months or a year with play money, to make sure your bets match what actually occurred so you feel more secure about that volatility within the game. Somebody may come along and say, "My God! Why would you only want a 5–8 percent return? I can get you 15 or 20 or even 30 percent in options." If you want to put 1 or 2 percent of your money into a speculative account and actively trade and gamble, fine. While in a few cases it can be viable and possibly even lucrative over time, I prefer to simply call it speculative entertainment, or gambling. It's just for so-called fun.

Although there are a few individuals who seem to do quite well speculating with such zero-sum-game approaches, most don't. With this approach, the net change in wealth is zero in the overall market. I prefer non-zero-sum game approaches, where all parties win and there is growth in the overall market.

If you are only speculating with a small percentage of your total portfolio, you aren't overly emotionally reactive when you gain or lose money, you're not concerned about any potential loss, you feel exceptionally secure, and you're still going to save and reach your outcome by more conservative methods, then I say you are in a position to entertain yourself by gambling a bit.

I prefer not to distract myself from my primary source of income by actively gambling. I prefer a patient, methodical, and more objective or executive approach.

If you want to give a small portion of your money to somebody that speculates in options, fine. Just know that it may be going along well for two or three years and crash. In gambling, probabilities are generally against you. The market can be like a gambling casino, where the odds are not generally in your favor. The laws of probability are in the casino's favor, even though the **house edge** varies significantly among the different casino games, or in this case, the investment classes.

Here is the problem with gambling: If you win and you win again, guess what happens? You tend to drop your more methodical objective strategy and assume, "I have some form of special awareness. I've got a secret formula. Somehow I've figured it out. Nobody else has got this answer. Now I'm going to borrow from my savings or margin account to put into more leveraged speculations." Again pride can come before the fall.

A Tale of Andrew

Let me share a story about a gentleman named Andrew in New York. He was a doctor. I met him in the early 1990s. When I first began consulting for him, he had $120,000 saved and invested and about $60,000 in cash, which was smart and stable. He had about $20,000 sitting in New York municipal bonds, which is very smart, because there are no taxes on yields from municipal bonds. He was earning about 5.8 percent on these. In his tax bracket, that is a net of about 9 percent, according to its tax equivalent yield: a very decent return on his money. He also owned $40,000 worth of shares in the Standard & Poor's 500 index.

I consulted with him. I increased his savings with the quarterly FAST approach, and he kept his savings in money markets, municipal bonds, and his investments in the stock index. He was saving about $5,000 a month. He was growing his practice faster and got up to $780,000 net worth over the next few years. His goal was to reach $1 million the next year. This was around 1998 to 1999.

During this time, the tech sector of the stock market and Nasdaq were climbing and starting to accelerate with irrational emotional exuberance. Andrew started to hear from some of his friends who were "killing it" speculating: everybody else was getting double-digit figures in day-trading the stock market. So Andrew took a portion of his hard-earned cash savings and bought some stock in Cisco, a technology company. He put something like $20,000 into Cisco. It jumped to $80,000 in a relatively short period of time. It doubled. It doubled again. He said, "Why am I in bonds? I made more money in this one Cisco investment than I have in all of my bonds." So he took $500,000 of his cash, bonds, and stocks and started to practice day trading, not actually realizing the capital gains taxes he exposed himself to by selling. At that time when you day-traded, you had to pay for the buy and sell, as well the taxes for short-term capital gains. You're paying the maximum tax bracket, and you're gambling. Andrew did this with a large portion of his portfolio.

Andrew went from $780,000 to $1.2 million, and he started getting a bit cocky. He started thinking, "Man, this is great. I'm not going to follow that more patient and methodical Demartini approach. I'm not going to follow that savings cushion regimen. I'm going for it. I'm going to become a day trader and private money manager, and I'm going to make millions doing this." He let his clinical practice nearly die. The emotional dopamine high of quick returns activated his subcortical amygdala more than his forebrain's executive center. He was in the get-rich-quick lane of immediate gratification.

Then the spring crash of 2000 hit. Guess what happened? Andrew lost over $1 million of his money when the Nasdaq plummeted nearly 80 percent. He had $240,000 left over. He was so stressed that he lost some of his hair. But he had gotten a taste of the pleasures and pains of gambling mania. He no longer appreciated his practice and did not want to go back to the basics and build a stable foundation once again. The high made him impatient, and he wanted to quickly stop his bleeding and recover his money as fast as possible. He was now vulnerable to almost any get-rich-quick scheme being offered.

Unfortunately, he'd been burned, and it was painful to go into the market, but he wasn't appreciating his practice, so he was really stuck. He broke his more conservative strategy because he got to experience a get-rich-quick high and later fall. He next tried to learn gimmicks and get-rich-quick schemes in options and futures, with so-called insurance calls and puts. He earned some of that money back, but it cost him seven years to recover.

Do you see why I'm encouraging you not to speculate until you have built up your savings cushions and developed a more conservative investing strategy first, and then only with a small portion? If you temporarily make a quick killing by speculation, it can be as distracting as losing, because you might get so elated that you foolishly start to think you're smarter than the market and can intellectually function beyond all of the known statistics. That's usually when you get bitten by subjective blindness.

Offshore Havens

You have no doubt heard about offshore tax havens. People say that you can avoid taxes by taking your money offshore. There's no doubt that there are legitimate tax structures that legally allow you to reduce and avoid, but not evade, your taxes this way, particularly if you have foreign source income and do not need to repatriate your income or capital gains for a while.

There are ways of accumulating your earned assets off-shore. When you have at least $250,000 to $500,000 net assets saved and then invested, and you earn this amount annually, it's probably worth sitting down with a tax accountant or tax attorney to discuss the legal possibilities. But it's important to make sure the program really matches your lifestyle and life objectives, because sometimes the laws will change and you may be occasionally redoing the legal structures. There are hidden costs, which can add up, as well as advantages.

There's nothing illegal about working for an offshore company; people do that quite often. I previously was one of the trustees of a holding company called International Celebrities. It was not a foreign-controlled corporation, since 80 percent of the other trustees were from the tax haven and managed and made financial decisions for the company. The company could hire me to do a seminar and have me flown to some international destination. The promoter or sponsor would pay the holding company directly offshore. They would pay me a moderate fee for doing that presentation, and they and I would leave the majority of the earned income in the offshore banking and investment account. The money would sit there, growing in a tax-free environment. Nevertheless, if they and I agreed to repatriate a portion of that money later in life, I would then pay the corresponding income or capital gains taxes on it.

This approach is perfectly legal. As long as you're not controlling it, it's called a *controlled foreign corporation*: a CFC. If you have too much control over it, it is then considered taxable income each year that it is earned. It would then be classified as a non-CFC, so you will pay taxes and fill in the proper tax forms each year. So the account would need to be structured properly, and you would require foreign source income, because you can't send money over there from this country without paying an income or a short or long-term capital gains tax. With this, along with taxes on interest, you're right back where you started, so this kind of account is not worth setting up unless you meet the ideal criteria. Full disclosure is also required by U.S. tax authorities. But if you have foreign source income, a non-CFC is one way of reducing taxes legitimately, because it's not really your money until it is brought into the U.S.: you're just working for another offshore tax-advantaged entity.

When my wife passed away nearly twenty years ago, I discontinued the offshore structure, repatriated the money, paid the corresponding income and capital gains taxes, and restructured my finances. Laws and rules can change, so what at one time may be advantageous at another may not be.

Today I simply and automatically pay my share of the estimated taxes weekly into a separate tax account and pay the tax authorities quarterly.

In any case, it's worth talking to a tax accountant who really knows that business. But this is only the case when you have enough annual income and start paying enough taxes that the amount that you'll save is worth the effort and extra costs of the specialists and corresponding legal structures, because it's going to cost you thousands of dollars to set such a system and structure up. If you're not making enough money to make it worth your tax savings, it's not worth considering or doing.

I suggest that you start with the basics. When you've got about $250,000 to $500,000 and you're earning at least $250,000, the amount of taxes you're paying is substantial enough to make it time to talk to a tax accountant or tax attorney. You'll have some costs in structuring and managing this account, but it may be preferable to paying some unnecessary taxes.

With some structures involving irrevocable trusts, the money is not exactly your money anymore. It's called a trust, because you are trusting somebody else to control and manage the money. By the way, it's important to be sure that's there's a real, legitimate trustee or company on the other end, or they could take off with your money. If you go to the Caribbean Islands, you'll see many banks on the streets. Some of them are shells; they don't really exist. They're just a 10 x 10–foot room with a sign that says "National Bank" or some other pseudonym. In reality, some of them are pseudobanks, advertised through the Internet, and they get people's money without anything behind them. They're shells. They're nothing. Billions of dollars are funneled into various structures in this way, because people can get greedy and don't want to pay their fair share of taxes to the government or tax authorities.

Use only legitimate authorized financial organizations for setting up trust structures. Have the individuals who set the structure up guarantee in writing that it is perfectly legal and have tax authority confirm it. It's wise to make sure your offshore tax haven account is legitimate. Make sure you do your due diligence, and confirm that it is a legal structure with your county's tax authorities before transferring any funds.

At any rate, it's wise to make sure the attorney will sign a piece of paper saying, "I authorize this as a legitimate and legal structure, and if there is a problem with the government here and there are penalties, I will be accountable." Then you know that individual is going to be legit. Tax avoidance is legal and wise. Tax evasion is not and can cost.

Currency Speculation

There are also ways of currency speculating. At one point in the late 1990s, Australia had a currency down to one Australian dollar to 49 U.S. cents. When my late wife and I saw that, we figured that it was probably a low. So we bought some Australian properties, figuring that we could get $2 million worth of property for every U.S. $1 million we invested.

Later in the next decade, the Australian dollar went up to par: one Australian dollar was equal to one U.S. dollar, meaning that our investment had appreciated by 100 percent. During that time, the real estate market went up another 50 percent, and we sold some of those properties, so we would be able to take advantage of both the currency market and the real estate market and double our money in just a few years. We moved a small to moderate percentage of our assets over to take advantage of the double whammy, and we made a bit of extra money in a reasonable time. But it wouldn't be prudent to do this with too much of the only money you had.

It you're buying foreign investments, it might be wise to be moderate the percentage of your portfolio in foreign, international, or global accounts. Check the history of the currency fluctuation differences in advance. When your county's market goes down, somebody else's market may be going up and vice versa, which could be used as a hedge against your country's or their country's fluctuating currency. So it could be wise to have a portion of each of your investment classes in international funds.

Real Estate

Of course, there are many different forms of real estate saving and investing. The value of a high-quality house that you use as a primary residence may or may not be considered a forced form of savings, depending upon whether the value of the house goes up and you build equity fast enough. Yet your primary residence may not fully be an asset; it can be a liability. In some cases, it can be taking more money out of your pocket than it is putting in. Generally, I prefer to consider your primary residence as a lifestyle cost more than as an actual investment.

Investing and speculating in the real estate market is quite different. In some cases, you're just buying a developer's idea; there's not even a full plan yet. Someone approaches you and says, "We're going to build a development, and we're looking for people that want to invest in it. You'll get it for a really great price if you buy now. It is really a speculation. When we get enough people who are willing to put some money up, we'll go forward." During an up market, a bank will probably support the project; it will pay for part of the development; you and other speculators will pay for part. As long as the market is on an up trend, and everybody looks as if they're going to make some money, it's considered a win-win. If the market goes down and the bank says, "Sorry, we're going to demand the deposit or interest payment money," and you don't have the savings cash cushion for it, you'll have to pay all the costs, including maintenance and taxes. Then you will be responsible to find somebody to lease it. You may get stuck with more cash outflow than inflow, at least initially. Be sure you run the numbers in advance and consider and mitigate your true potential risks under worst case scenarios.

To reiterate a previous point, during an up market, you think, "The rewards are worth the risks." The drawback is that you may blind yourself and think you can do that indefinitely. You raise your lifestyle and expenditures, as well as overleverage, which can trap you. If the market goes down, you are wise to have plenty of savings, new income, or an accessible cash cushion ready to handle the repercussions. If you have that in place and you're playing the game brilliantly, you're less likely to have a setback and become distressed. You can ride out the ups and downs and capitalize in the real estate market on the way up again by thinking over the long term. But if you play in that league without an accessible cash cushion, you're taking a potential risk. In fact, the market usually goes down when the banks become less regulated, lax, and optimistic, and everybody else is getting into the market because of emotional exuberance or blind elation.

I'm often asked how to think about home renovations. Say you are buying a house for $450,000. You know that adding an extra kitchen, bathroom, or bedroom is going to cost you $60,000, but it's going to add $100,000 to the value of your house; in that case, it can be classified as a potential investment. If you overcapitalize so that you now have the biggest house on the block even though it's not going to get any more than the average house, you can class the expense as lifestyle. Lifestyle is anything that depreciates; savings and investment are anything that appreciates.

It's also valuable to override your impulsive, immediate gratification, or infatuation responses. Sometimes you become infatuated with a purchase. If you hold back and not rush on a purchase, wait a week or two or more, and start saving a bit towards it, you'll find out how important it is to you. If it still is, you've got the additional money now; you can still buy it. But if you had just gone along with the initial impulse, afterward you could say, "Oh my gosh, what'd I do?" This approach gives you a cushion to prevent impulse purchasing, because impulse purchasing can cost you. Be sure you follow a checklist and do your due diligence on any property you are considering investing in.

Diversification

You may remember the fiasco of the Enron energy company around the turn of the century. Almost everybody investing in Enron lost some if not most of their fortunes, because many of them had all their money in that one single company. They violated one of the basic laws of sound investing: *diversification*. It's extremely wise to diversify. But I am not referring to overdiversification and dilution.

The late Charlie Munger of Berkshire Hathaway was once asked if he was well diversified or whether he could select only a few stocks and still do very well. He stated he could own just a few stocks and do very well. But this statement could be misleading to some newcomers. The few stocks he was referring to were conglomerates holding many other companies and their subsidiaries. For instance, owning shares of stock in Berkshire Hathaway really means you own stocks in sixty-five companies, each of which includes subsidiaries totaling into the hundreds. So holding just this one stock is being well diversified. And the few stocks he was referring to also were conglomerates structured the same way, so hundreds of stocks were included in his portfolio. So what seemed like a few was actually many.

I don't want to teach you speculation before you've earned the right to it. Suppose you came to me and said, "I've got $10 million of capital in savings, bonds, and stocks; I've got them providing relatively decent returns that I can turn over and liquidate tomorrow. I'd like to buy a million-dollar property and start investing in the real estate market." I'd say, "Fine, great; you've earned the right to play in the game." But without looking at your savings, bond, and stock holdings and their returns, I cannot be sure whether it is wise to liquidate and convert them into real estate. I would need to see what quality of real estate you are buying and where, and would have to run the numbers and determine the tax consequences of selling your current assets to buy the new real estate asset to see if it potentially is a wise move.

But if you say, "I've got $28,000; I'd like to borrow another $35,000 and put all that into this one piece of property" at the peak of the market, when everybody else is doing it, I'm going to tell you, "I wouldn't do it." I'd rather you have liquid capital saved as a reserve—guaranteed money—rather that a possibly overpriced property, unless it is an exception for a long-term buy.

At that point, I'd suggest that you save for your house. You can buy a house when you've got some money saved for the deposit and enough income to support the monthly payments and to save and invest on top. On average, the monthly house payment would ideally be no more than 25 percent of your steady average monthly income. In other words, if you're making $10,000 a month and your house payment is $2,500, you can afford it. If you're making $5,000 a month and your payment is $1,250, you can afford it. But if your total income is $5,000 and your house payment is $4,000, you would be probably foolish to buy; it's too much for that income, unless your income is about to go up. You would hopefully not qualify for a loan; otherwise the banks are not doing their job regulating such foolish transactions.

Like the other asset classes and sectors, the real estate sector has segments. Comparatively stable and easily accessible real estate investments that can be purchased across the various real estate segments are called *real estate investment trusts*, or REITs. These are tax-advantaged companies that own and typically operate income-producing real estate or related assets, enabling individual investors to participate in them at lower initial costs and through dollar-cost averaging. Again, I don't recommend going here before you have first saved your initial cash cushion and you have earned the right to risk.

Some real estate segments include commercial real estate, residential properties, retirement villages, personal homes, condominiums, and duplexes. On average, every segment has minor to moderate dips every decade or so and larger fluctuations over longer periods. This smaller cycle goes through four phases: recovery, expansion, hypersupply, and recession. If you're diversified across the segments and classes, you have the highest predictability of making a more predictable, yet moderate return.

If you've paid off your house completely, the equity accumulated is now partly an asset, though the house still has depreciating repair costs as well as land and other taxes, and it is still not producing cash flow unless it is turned into a rental property. You're not making mortgage payments anymore. Now you can look at your other income, including your passive investment income and your active earned income or borrowed income from equity in your primary residence. Since you are no longer paying on your primary residence, you may consider buying another piece of property, but the thinking here is similar. If the market went down and you were stuck with that mortgage and costs, could you afford it, with or without a renter? It is wise to consider all the common expected and unexpected costs that will emerge when leveraging in real estate.

If you become elated or manic about your investment, that's a sign you're not ready for it. If you go around telling everybody about how great it is and how excited you are, that's a warning. If you're either elated or depressed—you're not able to manage your emotions—you're not truly ready to manage that level of operation in finances. If you get manic and can't see the downsides, you're about to learn a lesson. It's a great idea to have a more emotionally balanced orientation. Every class, sector, and segment has pros and cons, but if you earn the right to risk, you can earn the right to handle those emotional states. When you are stable, you are steady and strategic rather than emotional and impulsive.

I had a few setbacks along these lines. Once, when I first learned the difference between investing and speculating, I put more than 10 percent of my portfolio into a deal: the developers said they were going to be building a new racetrack just on the edge of the city of Houston. Because the people involved in it had a lot of wealth, I thought, "If I'm hanging out with some of those wealthy guys I'm going to do what they do and receive a great return."

Instead of limiting my speculation to 10 percent of my portfolio, I put in a higher percentage into the deal and give it to the developer for the racetrack. It took him two extra years to get the racetrack deal finalized: he got caught in municipal bond challenges and political issues over the gambling. From this experience, I learned not to break strategy, not to try to get rich quick, to do more due diligence, to know whom I am dealing with, and to do business with people who are more governed and integral and are not just out to make a quick buck.

I went back to the basics and continued saving, investing in more quality investments, and became even more long-term oriented and patient. When the eighties came along, interest rates and returns were very high, and I was starting to accumulate some money. By the time the nineties came along, I was doing really very well.

During the early to mid-1990s, I had the opportunity to provide consulting services for a rapidly growing and emerging Internet website development company. Normally I was paid upfront in total for my speaking or consulting services. In this case, I was offered a smaller than normal consulting fee along with some shares in the growing company, and I decided to do it. The company skyrocketed, and the stock share price made a 45 percent rise the first month, another 25 percent rise in the second month, and another 30 percent rise in the third month. On paper, it temporarily appeared that being paid in this fashion was a win. This went on for about five years. So I thought this was an amazing opportunity, even though I was allowed to sell them after a minimum period. Then during a nearly 80 percent tech sector correction in the spring of 2000, the market turned around, and that stock dropped to around $1 a share. My stomach went into a bit of a knot. Nearly the entire so-called accumulated gains of the original speculation disappeared. I thought I was ready for that. I was ready for it to grow; I just wasn't ready for it to disappear. I realized how easy it was to fool yourself on your true risk tolerance. Even though the total investment was under 10 percent of my total portfolio, I still had an emotional reaction, since I had never experienced such a drop in such a short period of time in any one investment. I eventually sold my shares and received a moderate gain, but not more than I probably would have gained just receiving my full consulting fee and investing my normal amount using more conservative strategies.

In short, it's generally wise not to invest more than 10 percent of your net worth in any one company per sector, per class. It's wiser to diversify a bit across classes and sectors or through larger holding conglomerates or indices.

Active and Passive Funds

Now let's add another complicating factor. Regardless of class or sector, you have passive and active approaches to investing. The passive investment approach invests in stock *index funds*. The active investment approach invests in actively traded stocks or stock *mutual funds*. The difference has to partly do with the speed and quantity of trading.

Passive investing in index funds involves buying and holding preselected quality stocks with low or infrequent turnover rates. Generally lower costs are involved. Actively traded stock shares or stock mutual funds involves money managers actively engaged in buying and selling stocks more frequently, trying to beat the passive index fund benchmark returns. They have generally more costs involved. They do not beat the passive funds very often.

Index fund have small turnovers of buying and selling stocks. They usually buy a stock or a collection of stocks and, say, hold it in a bundle for years or even decades. Index funds are available for every class and sector. You can also buy a diversified index fund, which goes all the way up the classes and across the sectors. I invite you to consider investing in a diversified index fund, like the S & P 500 or the Dow Jones Industrials index fund in the United States. There is little to do, the cost ratios are lower, and the returns are historically competitive or greater than with active funds. The process is simple, and the funds can be purchased periodically and automatically.

Almost every investment company offers such index funds. There are some great ones that have the top fifty or 100 or 500 or 2000 companies. There are the S & P 500 index funds: they buy what the Standard & Poor's rating company lists as the 500 largest companies in America. Other funds buy indexes of the top 100 or 500 companies, which have stood the test of time and have great fundamentals and quality management. They have large capitalization, and if you put your money into them, you have a high probability of a certain amount of return over a period of time, say twenty-five years. One year the return may be negative. The next year it may be positive—2, 15, 20 percent. But overall these funds give you predictable returns according to their respective classes and their means. Historically, money markets make 4 to 6 percent per year. Bonds make 6 to 8 percent. Stocks make 8 to 10 percent. Thus each class has an average 2 percent increase in returns over the previous one.

Benjamin Graham, Warren Buffett's teacher and the father of value investing, looked at the long-term haul of all the people that speculated, all the people that invested, and all the people that saved. The people who divided their money half into savings and half into investing ended up with more yields in the long run than the speculators. They were more stable and patient. Financial wealth building involves deferred gratification and self-governance.

I knew a lady who was seventy-two years old. She and her late husband had saved $1,200,000. She was living moderately on her retirement income and was doing relatively well, but her money was not growing as fast as she wanted. She wanted to raise her lifestyle. She went to a seminar in Mexico on how to set up offshore trusts to avoid paying taxes to the government, accelerate your growth of money, and get rich quicker. She unwisely put a portion of her life savings into the recommended investment. On paper, she initially appeared to make 10 percent return in her first three months. "Wow!" she thought, "over 40 percent return in a year!" If she kept compounding this growth, she could quickly be very wealthy. She decided, "At this rate, if I put all my money in, I could make millions." She put nearly her entire nest egg in. The con woman who was receiving the lady's funds and her team moved off to the Caribbean Islands with her money and that of many others. The lady never saw her money again. It was a Ponzi con scheme. The lady's life savings was gone in a matter of months.

If it is too great to be true, it probably is. Getting rich quick has its vulnerabilities, and it can challenge your emotional stability. Patience is a virtue.

I've consulted with some people over the years who have lost nearly their entire fortunes with those types of con games. I don't want you to lose your fortune.

If, of course, you start and rapidly scale up an amazing, efficiently managed, highly profitable company that truly serves ever greater numbers of people, then getting wealthy more rapidly might be doable. But it is rare.

Put your money into savings and quality investments, and leave it there. Don't turn it over, don't try to time the market, and don't try to think you're smarter than the market. You're either a mathematical genius or an idiot to think you're going to beat the market consistently. Even the most skilled have a hard time doing so. Few if any have beaten the benchmark returns consistently for years. Anyone who tells you they're going to do it is either consciously or unconsciously misleading you. They're usually just telling you about the one time they did.

Like the lotto, the lottery, and the casino, speculative investments are not designed in your favor. Why would you want to put your money into areas where the odds are against you, gambling when you don't need to in order to build lasting financial wealth and freedom?

Overinvesting in Your Business

A man in Denver once told me, "I don't invest in anybody else's business. I return or invest all my earned income back into my own business."

"So you have no substantial savings cushion, and no other outside investments?" I said. "You just keep putting all of your earnings back into in your business, and you're hoping to sell that business and then have your fortune."

"Yes."

"So that means your heart's not into your business long-term. You're sort of a serial entrepreneur. You're going to rapidly build it and sell it."

"Yeah."

"Do you think you might be taking quite a bit of a risk? You've got all your eggs in one startup, penny stock, high-risk basket. You've got little to no liquidity, no demonstrated margin. Tell me, would you want to buy a business that has no consistent proven margin and no reserves?"

"No."

"Why would you expect somebody else to do that? If they see that you've got a year's worth of liquid capital in that company that's paying you a significant sum of money with a decent price/earnings ratio, you're going to be able to sell that a lot more easily than if you just keep putting all your monies into the business, with no margin. You might want to consider putting a little into both. If you keep a business on the edge, who's going to want to buy it except another overly optimistic gambler? The intrinsic value of the company is quite low."

It's prudent to guarantee your financial wealth. As Warren Buffet once stated" "Rule number one: don't lose your money. Rule number two: don't forget rule number one."

If you keep trying to get rich quickly because you hear about somebody else who has, you're setting yourself up for very high probabilities of falling back down. Financial wealth is a probability game. The principles I'm outlining here have been gradually worked out for decades, so I'm not telling you anything that's new, but I can assure you they are sound. Sure, there are a few exceptions that make fortunes seemingly overnight: having a big win while speculating, which is hard to consistently duplicate; building a great company that truly serves vast numbers of people, which generally takes years of dedication and team building; inheriting a fortune, which has its drawbacks; or lotto, which has its disasters.

I recommend that you build your wealth layer by layer, step by step, strategically, methodically and patiently. I prefer that you maximize your probability of becoming financially wealthy over time; I can't guarantee it the other, get-rich-quick way.

Man in a Pit

Let me tell you about a gentleman who attended the "Secrets to Financial Mastery" seminar program I presented in the 1990s. He was a broker in the options pit in New York. At one moment, he had a net worth of $11 million in his personal portfolio, then he would be down by $2 million, and then he'd be up by $4 million. And then down and up again. He had an extremely volatile dynamic—very much a risk taker.

When he was up, he'd fly to Europe for an extravagant weekend vacation. He would live a high, fast-lane life, wine, dine, rent private jets, and attend debauched parties. Then he'd have losses, and he would come down and be depressed and reclusive. He repeatedly had girlfriends that were interested primarily in spending his money when he seemed to have it and who dumped him when he lost significant sums. He had no checks and balances on his volatility and was manic and then depressed. If his highly speculative "investments" had major gains, he got high and didn't moderate his buying or selling of some of them; if they had major losses, he got low; he didn't have a sufficient savings reserve to buy opportune value stocks. He was foolishly run by his subcortical amygdala or desire center, not his wiser medial prefrontal cortex, or self-governing executive center.

At one point during the seminar, this man broke down and cried. He was in the pits—the New York options pit. You can make a lot of money quickly there, and you can lose a lot quickly. Sometimes people commit suicide when they lose after becoming addicted to the high when they assume they have gained.

I asked this man how much money had passed through his hands over the eleven years he had been investing.

"It's $72 million."

"What is your net worth now?"

"$400,000. That's where I'm at right now. I recently lost my last fortune." He did a big deal in options on margin and lost a huge sum of money. He had most of his eggs in one basket and did not consistently follow a methodical strategy. After his last big win, he exaggerated his skill and assumed he could once again outdo the market, so he bet big and overleveraged on margin. The market sector crashed, and the margin call wiped him out. But this time he seemed to ready for a change.

"Will you help me manage my emotional state so I can rebuild stable financial wealth again?" he asked me. "I think I learned my lesson finally."

"Sure," I said.

We set up a system starting with his $400,000, and he was not allowed to use more than $40,000 in the game. If he made a profit on it, which he often did—$2,400 or $3,000—he took portions of that and stuck it back in the market, but not more than 10 percent beyond the amount he started with. He saved and then invested the difference into more conservative passive investments. Over the next five years, he was back up but with more stability and a methodical strategy to follow. He accumulated $7.5 million in stairstepping investments and was trading with about $2 million in the market: about 20 percent of his whole financial portfolio.

He eventually married. If his caring wife saw him in a manic state when he came home due to a decent return or the day, she would have him call Dr. Demartini, because she didn't want to be the one that was always nagging him. He might pay a few dollars to get on the phone with me for a few minutes, but I would neutralize him to stabilize his mood. We had a system of checks and balances. I would give him the drawbacks if he was up, the benefits if he was down. He would go back into the game the next day with a balanced perspective. He no longer got too high or too low. He was methodical, following a more proven and patient strategy for his short-term and now long-term investments.

Nine years later, this man had more money and more stability than he did in the previous eleven years. He no longer had huge rises or falls. He was averaging between 27 and 30 percent annually off his investments before taxes, giving him the potential to reach $100 million through automated investing and compounding by the time was seventy-two.

6

Money on the Brain

For the last forty-six years I have been fascinated by the human brain and mind, and I have studied neurology and psychology; in fact, I recently wrote a 1,000-page textbook titled *The Brain, Nervous System, and Consciousness*, and in it I shared something quite interesting.

Your single sensory and motor peripheral neurons can function together by means of a simple monosynaptic reflex arc or stimulus-response: often with an all-or-nothing, above or below threshold action or graded potential.

Once you enter your central nervous system—the next level of organization of your brain and nervous system beyond your single neurons, peripherally and in the spinal cord—it, again, operates largely with all-or-nothing responses, although with some small refinements. Now the central interneurons can grade and modify your simple reflex responses.

When you rise up into your brain stem, which has still more interneurons, associations, or refinements; it begins to have the capacity to modulate your basic reflexes with some degree of foresight and reflection.

As you go even higher, your cerebellum and subcortical and cortical areas of the brain all work to coordinate and govern your simple, more basic reflexes. If there is damage in the higher centers of the brain, the reflexes can become spastic. If the higher centers are intact, you have more refined movement responses, over which you have conscious control.

Refinement of control continues progressively from the brain stem to the basal ganglia, the limbic brain, and the cortex. Finally, the medial prefrontal cortex—the most forward, highest, and most advanced region in the neocortical brain—has command over the maximum number of interneurons, associations, and connections, which enable you to have highly refined, reflective actions as responses.

The greater the numbers of interneurons in the higher cortical areas, the more reflective, governed, and reasonable, that is, objective your actions become. The greater the number of interneurons, the greater the number of optional responses, and the greater the probability of a governed or mean distribution of response.

Under stress, we tend to regress: we go back down into our evolutionary past and react with a more basic reaction, on an ungoverned, all-or-nothing basis. You may have observed extreme stress or rage in yourself like an exterior witness. You're watching yourself, but you can't do much about it because you're responding with all-or-none, fight-or-flight reflexes. When you calm down and are no longer under perceived distress, you have a more refined, articulate, communicative process, and you think things through.

In short, the highest centers of the brain are more governed and poised, and the lowest centers of the brain are very reactive for survival responses. The neurons designed for distress responses are of large diameter, so they conduct rapidly. As a result, we have fast impulsive responses when we're perceiving ourselves under stress.

Stress and Volatility

As you progress in your economic or financial wealth building development, it is wise to follow your brain development process in an inverse fashion. When you are inexperienced and most vulnerable and reactive initially, it is prudent to have your financial portfolio most stable and conservative. When you are more experienced and evolved in your financial understanding, you can handle more volatility, because you are more objective and resilient and much less likely to react (although you may still choose not to engage in more volatile investments).

Financially, distress can be simply your response to extreme market volatility. If the market goes extremely high or extremely low, you can unintentionally become elated or depressed, because you've exaggerated or minimized what's actually going on, and you're highly vulnerable to emotional reaction. If you know how to integrate and balance your perceptions, you don't react and can handle volatility.

You will fear the loss of that which you infatuate with (gains and up markets) and you will fear the gain of that which you resent (losses and down markets). But remember, you make money from deposits from the past when the market goes up, and you make money from deposits in the future when the market goes down—if you just keep buying and become a net buyer. Either way, you will make money according to the market and class mean over time.

Most people think that they're ready to handle extreme market volatility when they're not. The second the market goes up, they grow elated, and they think they're really doing well. They become extroverted and tell everybody about their gains, which is often a sign they're about to have a correction or fall. Whenever you're overexuberant emotionally and in a manically elated state regarding your finances, you know what's about to happen: you are at the accelerating phase, near the top of the market cycle. Pride before the fall.

Because your brain is set up in a hierarchical fashion, the more you have a poised or balanced perception of the market, along with a state of gratitude, the more you function at the higher cortical levels; the more you have emotional volatility, ingratitude, and distress, the more you function at lower subcortical levels.

When you're a new saver and investor and functioning down in lower subcortical levels, it can be wise to build yourself a stable financial system with few or no fluctuations. When you know how to master your emotions more because you have built layers of savings cushions and conservative investments, it's then wise to go ahead and invest more in higher risk-reward ratios and possibly speculate, because you can tolerate the fluctuations. You have earned the right and learned the strategies to handle risk. That stabilizes and yet expands your risk tolerance. As long as you have three to six months or more of adequate liquid savings cushions to handle any unpredictable events, you will stay more strategic and unwavering in your pursuit of patiently building financial wealth.

Mystery of the Logos

When I was about eighteen, my dream was to become a master of my life and to study the natural laws of the universe, exploring all the sciences, and the humanities, including physiology, psychology, philosophy, and theology. At the time I became interested in the *logos,* the reason, knowledge, and order of the universe. The logos was considered the principle source of all existence. According to the ancient philosophers and mystics, like Heraclitus and Empedocles, this source of all existence, the enlightening, loving order of the universe, gives rise to everything. There are many names for the logos: one used in today's cosmology is the *singularity point.*

Later, the study of the logos branched out into various ologies, or disciplines, each of which further splintered and subdivided into various fields of study or degrees of intelligence. I wanted to know what that primal field of intelligence, the source of existence, was, so I started studying the various ologies and finding the laws that were consistent in all of them. At this point I'm convinced that economics, finance, psychology, the study of the brain, and the study of business completely overlap in the principles and laws that apply to them. The more the disciplines you study, the more you see the overlapping confirmation of those laws, the more certainty you have about them, and the more you understand how they dictate the direction of your destiny through homeostatic feedback systems within and around you.

As a result, when I'm building my financial structure, I'm not thinking of it simply in economics; I'm thinking in terms of chemistry, biochemistry, physiology, neurology, psychology, theology, philosophy, and business sociology. I'm thinking in terms of the many different ologies that are woven together to make this process viable and fruitful as possible.

Economics as Exchange

Economics began with a simple process of exchange. Originally, it principally had to do with beads, shells, and then livestock. As society grew, it became increasingly inefficient to be moving sheep and cows around as instruments of exchange. The society moved to silver and gold, eventually creating coins. After a while, that too became cumbersome: thousands of coins were heavy to move and vulnerable to robbers. People in decision-making positions decided to make the money lighter. That was the beginning of paper money.

But even paper money became inefficient when it was a matter of transporting millions of dollars, which again were heavy and prone to theft. So society went to plastic: credit and later debit cards. Now we've gone one step further and have electronic money. We can transfer $1 million by computer or smartphone. Then we went one step further, on to photonics. Photonics means light. At this point, it's feasible to transfer money at the speed of light: 186,000 miles per second. Next will be simultaneous entangled quantum transfers and exchanges. Each form of exchange becomes more and more efficient.

Money is now actually digitized light. The true definition of money is the presence of light. That's similar to some ancient spiritual teachings. Isn't it interesting that economics uses terms that are essentially axiological and theological? Values, goods, and services. The mastery of economics and financial wealth building is a matter of mastering ourselves—our own internal psyche. That's why Warren Buffett says that until you can manage your emotions, don't ever expect to manage money.

Economic and financial management activities teach us to practice the skill of managing our own psyche as we awaken our inspired state and live out a self-actualized life. We're here to do what we love, love what we do, live an inspired life and assist others in doing the same. Economics is one of the ologies that assist us in self-actualization, awakening the presence of enlightenment in our self: it enables us to be present and in fair exchange with the world by communicating our values in terms of others' values for the sake of sustainability. Consequently, theology, sociology, axiology, economics, and neuroscience are all interwoven. There's no real separation between them except for a few bits of language. And knowing their languages allows us to communicate across those different ologies.

These interconnections all point to one truth: once we declare we are worth something and we are committed to it, the world within us and around us helps us readjust ourselves to accommodate our most inspired and meaningful mission. It's as if the world is waiting for us to declare our worth. It will test us. If we are wavering and hesitant, we get bitten to redirect us. If we go forward and follow our strategy without emotionalizing, we will progress. When we are congruent life is on the way. When we are not it seems to be in the way.

A vital part of the process is to add service. Your sense of fulfillment is closely connected to how much service to others you provide. Without service to others, there is no valuable source of income. You may have noticed that you feel more fulfilled and energetic at the end of an extremely productive and meaningful day. The day goes by quickly; you feel present all day long; you don't notice time and space; you feel that it all went smoothly. You feel energized and productive because you made a great,, rewarding income by serving and fulfilling the needs of other people.

Seven Forms of Immortality

Many individuals have a thirst for immortality. They have the desire to make a difference and leave a mark in the world. They often believe that they some form of consciousness or conscious expression that lives beyond their physical form. Across the world, some 95 percent of the world's population believe in an afterlife of some kind. We could call that spiritual immortality.

Immortality can be expressed in, or take on, seven forms, of which spiritual immortality is just one. We would also like to have mental immortality in the sense that we would like to pass on our knowledge to somebody else and be remembered for it beyond our life.

A third form of immortality involves the desire to pass a business, brand, or enterprise on to your children or a purchaser. We worked many years to build a system that produces income for people, and we would like pass it on to future generations.

Then we have a desire to have our family or offspring survive us. We want our children to outlive us.

Once, when my grandmother was ninety-seven, I asked her what it was like to be her age. "It's very challenging when you see your children dying before you," she said. "Outliving your children is not what you envisioned when you started." Two of her children had already died in their seventies. When she died at the age of 101, only two of her children survived her.

Next is social immortality: the desire to leave some impact on society beyond our lives. You want to be remembered by society. Don't you at least want to have at least one human being who remembers who you were?

There is also the desire for physical immortality. Wouldn't you like to still have a relatively vital, agile body when you're ninety, or maybe even when you are 100 or more?

Finally, we want financial immortality. We'd like to have our money outlive our mortal lives, leaving some behind for our children, or perhaps a philanthropic educational or charitable foundation.

7

How to Raise Your Lifestyle

If you would love to help scale up your business, and therefore drive your income up, one way to do so is to progressively increase your automated savings and then investments. You can do this by putting them into an organized, automated, and progressively accelerating or appreciating saving and then investment accounts The quality of the financial demand you put on yourself and your business will partly determine your business income supply.

One principle of the universe that is acknowledged by most scientists is the second law of thermodynamics, also called the principle of entropy. This is the tendency of material objects to go from ordered states and arrangements to disordered states and arrangements over time. The entropic arrow of time appears to demonstrate this. Entropy is sometimes called death physics.

In 1944, Nobel laureate Erwin Schrödinger wrote a book entitled *What Is Life?* and coined the term *negentropy* for the tendency of all living life forms and organizations to move in the opposite direction from entropy as they are alive and growing, moving from disorder to order.

This first law of entropy and its opposite, negentropy, also apply to economics and individual financial wealth building. If your financial house is not organized, it will automatically be consumed by lower-priority distractions or entropy in the form of unexpected bills and consumables that go down in value. Without uphill order and organization, there will be downhill disorder and disorganization.

The more order you bring to your business and financial house, the more business and income it will attract. Money is drawn from inefficiency to efficiency. People that value financial wealth building want to put their money where it flows in the direction of greater order and organization, where it appreciates in value. That is why the wealthy pay their savings and investments first and keep buying assets before unexpected bills and entropy erode their opportunity to do so. The poor pay themselves last and buy depreciating consumables. Entropy overrules them, so their potential financial wealth decays.

Similarly, every time you raise your expenditure on your consuming lifestyle, it's wise to raise your savings, investments, and tax payments by equal amounts. If you do this, you will continue to move forward with financial wealth building rather than backward with immediate gratification and consumable entropy. This practice will help you govern your purchases and make sure they are truly important and worth buying.

The more you raise your monthly lifestyle, the more savings and investments you will require to be able to passively pay for them to attain financial freedom. Deferred gratification builds it, immediate gratification can destroy your financial wealth building.

Here's another of my rules of thumb on raising lifestyle: see how you can get paid profitably for it. Let's say you're saving and investing $6,000 or $8,000 a month. You feel you're on track with building your appreciating assets, but you'd like to have a new car or some new furniture, or you'd like to take a little trip.

Again, you can ask yourself, how can I get handsomely or beautifully paid to acquire my new car, furniture, or trip? How do I go on a trip and get paid for it? Whatever you'd love to do, it's sensible to ask, "How do I do what I love and get profitably paid for it?" If you brainstorm, amazing ideas come into your mind on how to pull it off.

I opened up my second office in Houston for $10,000, and it was a fabulous office. First, I went to a place that sold business furniture, and I said, "I'm Dr. Demartini. You may have seen my television show." I was on television those days.

The salesman said, "Yeah, I have actually seen it."

"I've just opened up a new office, and I'm having a big open house. I'm curious: would you like to put your furniture on display in my office? I'm going to have a lot of people and media there. I will allow you to put your sales materials out, and I will stand up and make a comment about you as one of the people that have helped me in the opening of my new office. If you'd like to do it, I'd promote you. I'm very sure that you're going to get some business out of it. In return, I ask that I get ninety days interest-free on the furniture, and I'll pay it out as I go."

I also asked him, "If we sell furniture that evening, or if anyone from that evening or afterward who sees your furniture in my office comes into your showroom, may I receive 15 percent of the sale toward the payments of my new furniture?"

"Done." He delivered the furniture.

I had beautiful furniture in my new office. When I had the open house, I announced and recommended this man and his store. He sold many pieces of furniture from that evening on, because I had said, "This is the gentleman to buy your furniture from."

Then I went to an art gallery and did the same thing. I asked, "How have sales been?"

"They've been great," the dealer replied.

"Would you like to increase your sales?"

"Of course I would."

"I'm doing an open house, and I'm having the media, and there'll be up to 300 or 400 people there. If I were to have you put your signs up, showcase your magnificent art, and let them know about your gallery, would that be of value to you?"

"Absolutely."

"All you have to do is bring your finest art in. If people buy it right there, fabulous. If not, I will be buying some." I worked out a deal with them whereby I had magnificent art in my office, and I didn't have to pay a thing for it. We sold some of his art that evening, and over time he replaced what was sold, and I received some pieces off the 15 percent commission. It's all negotiation.

It's wise to think, "How can I get handsomely or beautifully paid to do whatever I love? How do I negotiate a deal in such a way that everyone wins too?" I can't just do exchanges where I win and they don't; both parties are to win. Sustainable fair exchange is what saves and earns money to be saved and invested.

As your financial assets continue to grow, new ideas and ways to earn more will pop into your head. Remember, I said if you have a thousand dollars, you get thousand-dollar ideas; if you have a million dollars, you get million-dollar ideas and million-dollar opportunities.

You may have noticed that if you concentrate on a certain client, customer, or patient, pull their name out of your inactive files, and read it, or just think about them, they will begin to mysteriously call, come by, or run into you. You can pull out old client, customer, or patient files and reactivate clients by visualizing them and concentrating on them. Ask, "What might I do for their birthday or anniversary?" Maybe call them if necessary.

When you do that, often these people will show up and become reactivated. You'll run into them at the grocery store, the gas station, or a restaurant, or they will just call. They'll say, "Oh, I was just thinking about you," and they'll be reactivated as clients.

The field of consciousness is a game of resonance. What you think about, you bring about. When you can't wait to get up and be of service to your clients, they can't wait to get up and be served.

People want to be loved for who they are. When you love them for who they are, they turn into who you love. Your clients, customers and patients are worth putting in your heart. By having them in your heart, you activate some form of non-local connection with them, and you resonate with them. Whenever you have someone on your mind and in your heart, you tend to bring them into your life.

The Law of Lifestyle Raising

Although I just mentioned it a few pages back, I would love to reemphasize the importance of forced savings and investments. It's wise to force your savings and then investments, no matter what.

Here's the law of lifestyle raising again: At some point, you may think, "I've been saving; I've been accelerating my saving and now investing; it's growing. I'm well on my way to building financial wealth. But right now, instead of only long-term gratification, I think I'd like to gratify one of my needs now."

No problem. Here's what I recommend. If you want to increase your lifestyle by $1,000 per month, all that is required is to know whether you're ready for it: "Am I willing to save or invest that same amount money per month, whatever that amount is? Since I also have to account for increased taxes as well, and they're probably 25 to 40 percent, am I ready to put the same amount into my taxes?" In other words, if you can save or invest the same amount and pay the same amount of taxes accordingly, you have earned the right to raise your lifestyle that same amount.

If for some reason you don't think you can afford all that, you can take what you think you can afford, divide it into three, and raise your lifestyle by one third, leaving the other two thirds for savings or investments and taxes. You're raising your lifestyle, but you're still progressing towards financial freedom. The next quarter you can do it again: you can raise your lifestyle by another third and put the other two thirds toward savings or investments and taxes.

I don't recommend you raise your lifestyle unless you can save or invest and pay the added taxes by an equivalent amount; because if you raise your lifestyle without raising your savings, investments, and tax payments to the same extent, you start stressing yourself with added lifestyle costs. But if you raise your savings, investments, and taxes equally, you feel, "I earned it." When you raise the savings or investments to balance out your lifestyle improvement, you receive more money to manage, because you're still managing money wisely; you just receive more money to build your financial wealth with.

This is a method of checks and balances to make sure that you've really earned the right to raise your lifestyle. Otherwise, you're prone to impulse buying and added entropy. Have you ever made an impulse buy and then questioned or beaten yourself up afterwards? Probably the purchase was enjoyable for a week or two, and after that it was not even meaningful.

A friend of mine bought a boat; it wasn't that expensive. For about three months, he used it almost every weekend. He burned the family out till they didn't want to even look at it. Then it sat out in the yard, deteriorating and depreciating. He hardly ever used it anymore.

By having this system of checks and balances, my friend would have probably been more moderate about the purchase, or it wouldn't have been as stressful, and he would have had the money to take care of the maintenance.

Before you impulsively buy immediate gratifying consumables that depreciate in value, you might want to ask yourself this set of eye-opening questions.

What is the total amount of money that I have earned during my entire life?

What is my total net worth at this current moment?

What percentage of all of the money that I have earned is now an asset, earning me a return?

Let's say that that percentage is 5 percent. Then it took you earning $200,000 to have $10,000 net worth earning you a return. So if you choose to buy a consumable item that depreciates in value that costs $5,000—say a new purse or outfit—you would be required to earn the equivalent of $100,000 to be able to buy that new purse.

But the $5,000 also could have been invested and turned into $10,000, $20,000, $40,000, then $80,000 over time with long-term compounding interest. So, depending upon your age, if you add these two factors together into the equation, the purse or outfit may be much more costly than first meets the eye.

Also, if you bought the purse or outfit with a credit card, you add even more costs to it. Buying a depreciating consumable with a credit card can be deceiving, since there is a separation between the pleasure of buying from the pain of paying. Whenever the bank separates these two poles of one transaction, you have less governance over what you buy, and you let your subcortical amygdala rule your decision-making.

When you buy on the spot with cash, the pain and the pleasure are simultaneous, so you are more thoughtful and buy with more executive center foresight rather than being impulsive, buying with desire center hindsight and later regretting it.

Travel Tips

If you do a bit of traveling and you're using a credit card or an American Express card that you pay off in full each month, it's valuable to have one that gives you travel miles. Similarly, it's wise to have hotel memberships that give you points for every hotel stay you stay in. So if I stay in a hotel, let's say for seven days, I get enough points to give me an extra day. I also use the American Express Centurion card, and I get mileage points and other perks. If I stay every two weeks on average, I get one free flight and a weekend stay in a hotel. When I look at the amount I save this way (assuming I was going to be taking the trip anyway because of my international professional speaking career), I stick it into savings and investments.

Whenever you stay in a hotel, it's prudent to ask for an upgrade. If the hotel is not full, they'll sometimes give it to you. It's always wise to ask what you want. The same is true in airlines. There's no risk in asking.

The same applies on the other end. A man came to me at a seminar one time and said, "I'd like to buy some of your CDs. If I bought everything you had, could I get a discount?"

"Absolutely," I said. Do I mind giving him a discount if he is buying in bulk? He bought $4,700 worth of my CDs and DVDs. I didn't mind giving him a specific percentage off.

Unconscious Money Motives

As you probably know, unless you reward yourself for your work and receive a sustainable fair exchange for your effort, you could burn out.

I once got a call from a doctor of chiropractic who had previously written a letter of recommendation for me to apply for professional school years before. He said, "This is Mark. I'd like to have my wife and I come and chat with you."

"Sure, absolutely." I felt honored, because he had been an mentor to me.

When they came into my office, he sat down. His wife started to cry, and he broke down. He said, "John, I'm here because I'm really afraid."

"Why?"

"I have seven children. I made a commitment to myself that every one of them would become a doctor of chiropractic." He came from a chiropractic family; his father was a chiropractor. "I've got one in chiropractic college and another in college, getting ready to enter into chiropractic college. My dream was to help them through their education, and I just don't have the required money." He started crying. He said, "It's killing me. I'm still in debt. I've never been able to get out of debt. I've worked now for all of these years, and I cannot see light at the end of the tunnel. I'd made a commitment to myself that I was going to help all of my children go to chiropractic college, but that's very expensive. That's thousands and thousands of dollars per year for their schooling and expenses. Even though they want to work to help out, my dream is to pay their way. And I feel like I'm letting my family down."

Mark burst into tears again. His wife was still crying, and he couldn't speak for a couple minutes. He said, "I almost feel like I would be more help to my family if I was dead with my insurance policy. I have actually been thinking of suicide. It means more than anything to me to see them finish professional school, but unless I can double or triple my income to cover their costs, there's no way I'm going to do that." He and his wife were afraid he was going to kill himself.

He said, "So I want your help. What can I do?"

And I thought, "There are options. You can kill yourself, kill your children; you could negotiate with the college to give you lower fees, you could split some of the costs with your children and have then participate in a work-study program. Or you can figure out a way of making more income and save and invest more."

He banged his head against the wall. People will bang their heads against the wall when they don't know how to go beyond their current self-imposed limits. Then they'll start to lie to themselves, saying, "I really don't want what I thought I wanted anymore. That's not really important to me." You have no idea how many people come to me and say, "It's not really important to me." I say to them, "If I could show you how to get what you say is not important to you without a major effort, would you be interested?"

"Oh, yeah."

When I give them a resonant and viable strategy, boom! They're on their way again. They really wanted it, but they lied to themselves. It's natural to have a desire to expand, but if we don't have a strategy for accomplishing it, we can sometimes lie to ourselves about what we really want. This why knowing your hierarchy of values and setting congruent objectives is so important.

Mark and I decided to come up with a strategy for generating more income and saving and investing more. He had not consistently saved and invested and didn't believe he could. Why? Because he paid his business first. He paid himself a little salary to live on, paid his taxes next, and had no savings. He was even behind on his taxes. The wealthy pay themselves first, because they place a higher value on themselves and on financial wealth building, and the impoverished pay themselves last, because they place a low value on themselves and on their financial future.

His hierarchy of values did not have business and financial wealth building near or at the top. He had education and family higher on his list. His hierarchy of values was creating his reality and destiny. Without a change of values, he was going to keep banging his head against the wall. Whenever you expect to live outside your current set of values and priorities, you will frustrate yourself to no end.

We worked together and did a value transformation process to raise business and financial wealth building higher on his list of values and began a forced automated saving and then investment structure for himself as well as automated his taxes, and we forced him onto a budgeted lifestyle, which wasn't excessive but enough to live more than comfortably. We also set up some of those savings in such a way that they were going to go for professional school, because I knew that was even more important to him than living. If I had not pushed him and his wife to have a shift in their values and manage their income more wisely and had not supported the change, they would have continued to get the same results.

I made him place wealth higher on his list of values by stacking up many benefits of doing the following six action steps that I have found common to most financially wealthy individuals.

1. Building a business that serves ever greater numbers of people.
2. Managing the business more effectively and efficiently to maximize profits.
3. Saving an ever progressive portion of the profits.
4. Investing in ever greater degrees of leverage by earning the right to risk.
5. Accumulating a fortune.
6. Having a greater financial cause for the purpose of building this fortune that leaves a legacy.

After a couple of consulting meetings that week, with some suggested action steps on how to grow his practice and income, by the end of his very first week, for the first time in his practice, Mark was able to transfer into his now automated saving system of $200 per week. Then a $2,000 check showed up unexpectedly that he had been waiting for from a personal injury case. It's as if the world economically rewarded him when he began to manage money wisely. Then checks for accounts receivable suddenly started to show up.

"Were you expecting those payments?" I asked.

"No."

"Then let's put them immediately into his new savings money market account."

Mark wasn't really far in debt. He still had small mortgages on his house, because he had borrowed against it a couple times. He only owed about $37,000, with another $20,000 in taxes, so he was only about $57,000 in debt; it wasn't a lot. In six months, nearly all of his debts were cleared. We had it almost all paid off, and one year later he had $40,000 saved and was current with his taxes and was automating all of his progressively increasing savings and passive index investments.

At that point Mark had gotten some investment leverage, and his goal was to save $65,000 the next year. He felt he had some life in him. He was on a roll again; he was like someone else, five years younger. He saw light at the end of the tunnel, and he was continuing to add more to the professional school fund for his children.

By the end of the second year, Mark definitely made more money and added more funds for his children's professional school. But then something happened. One night as he was eating dinner out with his family, celebrating being out of debt and beginning to see light at the end of the tunnel for his children to go to professional college, he suddenly choked on a piece of meat and died in a restaurant.

Part of Mark apparently just wanted the debt pressure off him. Because he had a million-dollar insurance policy, all of his children were able to go to and have now finished chiropractic college. Possibly because of some unconscious motive about what he truly wanted—which was having all of his children go to and finish professional school—he achieved his goal. Even though he had made significant financial progress, had become debt-free, and had begun his savings and investments and even school funding, he was apparently unconsciously still saying: "If I die, I am certain that all of my seven children will be able to attend professional school." (Of course, this assumed scenario is only a possibility, not a certainty.)

Maybe there is a hidden order in what we first imagine to be outer apparent chaos. Mark had another doctor as a business partner working side by side in his practice. This doctor had been like a brother to him and a large part of Mark's family, but was single and childless. He saved and invested much of his money and was well off. When Mark died, his business partner stepped up and declared to Mark's wife, "No matter what, I'll make sure that all seven kids go to and complete professional school." He eventually ended up in a relationship with Mark's wife. They got married and put most of the million-dollar insurance cash into some higher-quality investments, and he helped his previous partner's children all go to and complete professional school. All of them are chiropractors today. The oldest two learned from that experience, and upon graduating, they began saving and invested a large portion of their incomes. The father in a sense catalyzed their desire to become financially wealthy. Having financial challenges as a child can be a blessing and can sometimes light a fire for building financial wealth for the future.

The point is that we sometimes have unconscious motives. If it's easier to get our outcome by dying than by living, we may well die to get that outcome. Doctors know that patients sometimes have unconscious motives not to heal because they get too much affection and attention by not healing or they can avoid some unfulfilling responsibility. It sometimes starts when children use ailments to avoid a bully at school or with parents who dote over their children when they are sick or get minor injuries.

We sometimes have unconscious motives about what we love to do with our money, and because it is unconscious, we don't even realize it. Our hierarchy of values dictates our financial destiny. Our unconscious motives really consist of our list of values on our value systems. When we consciously try to live according to somebody else's value systems, our unconscious motives, based on our real value system, surface and manifest in our life regardless.

What many individuals think is vitally important to them often turns out not to be all that important. It does not stand the test of time as a true objective. Their lives demonstrate what their true value is, not necessarily what they wish it to be, fantasize about, or claim is truly important. Often these injected and conflicting values result from the comparison of themselves to others they admire and injected values from those they look up to.

In Mark's case, if I had addressed the unconscious motives, I might have gotten down to their core and origin and neutralized them. Instead, the family and I assumed that because he was starting to see light at the end of the tunnel, he was over the hump. But he choked on a piece of meat, and I don't think that was entirely by accident. I think it was the result of his unconscious motives, although of course I have no proof.

In any case, in a matter of just under two years, Mark was completely out of his debts, seeing light at the end of the tunnel, and moving upward financially. I believe if he would have kept up with his progressive, automated, and strategized saving and investment system for six more years, he could have gotten all of his sons through school and still had financial wealth building.

8

Money Management

When you manage money wisely, you start receiving more money to manage. Here's another simple action step that can help you build financial wealth: every time somebody pays for something that you were intending to buy—say a breakfast, lunch, dinner, or some other item—write down how much they just saved you. Whenever somebody takes me to a dinner that I had been expecting to buy, I ask them, "How much was that bill?" I write it down. Since I was ready to pay, I knew I could afford it, so I increase my savings by that amount that day or the next day. If you believe you could have paid for something but didn't end up doing so, that's a savings or investment opportunity. You'll be surprised: that will average hundreds if not thousands of dollars a month in some cases.

Whenever you receive unexpected income—or have been saved an expense that you were prepared to pay—take that amount and stick it in savings and investments. Many think that such small amounts are not significant, but they add up and compound over time. Piggy banks become "biggy" banks. It is not the amount that is most important as much as it is the habit of saving and investing.

Running a Budget

The purpose of a budget is not necessarily only to curtail or constrain your ungoverned spending. It is to also discover where you are prioritizing (and not prioritizing) your spending and where you can extract more savings and investment monies. When you manage money wisely and save and invest more, you end up with even more income coming in.

So it's a great idea to run a budget and master the art of governing yourself and becoming more efficient and prioritized. All that is essential is to look at where your accounts payable are going. It will blow your mind. You'll say, "Gosh, I can't believe I'm spending that amount on this." You'll immediately come up with strategies for being more efficient and extracting more monies that can go into savings and investments: "I don't know if I require that. I think I'll get a water filter instead of buying bottles of water." You'll think of different ways to save $50 here, $100 here, and another few hundred dollars will go into savings. In some cases, it can be in the thousands.

My dad did that years ago. We lived in the country, and we had to drive twenty or thirty miles every day to work. At one point he said, "I'm driving all the way over and all the way back to get gas." He calculated how much it was costing him just to drive to get gas, and said, "This is crazy." He got a license to bring wholesale gas onto his property and got a pump. He got 30 percent off the cost of the gas, and it was delivered to him. He saved time and money and invested the difference.

You want to ask yourself, "How can I live more effectively and efficiently?" You're not necessarily cutting out items of high priority, only low priority. The second you identify where you can save another $20, $50, $100, $500, or thousands, it's wise to stick it into savings and investments, so your money can work for you more than you work for it.

By prioritizing your expenses, you're merely making yourself more efficient and effective at managing money. You wouldn't imagine investing in a company that didn't have a budget or quarterly projection, and was not focused on maximizing product, or service income and minimizing costs, would you? All companies whose stocks you're buying are required to run quarterly projections of where they anticipate going for the next quarter. They are required to have a budget, and they are evaluated quarterly on how close they stick to that budget. Seldom does anyone or any company hit the exact target, or stay exactly on budget. Some go above it, some below it on different months. But overall, it's extremely important to have a budget to target your spending, cash flow, and reserves.

If for some reason your income goes over what is anticipated on the budget projection, you can take that additional amount earned and put it into a stabilizing savings cushion or directly into quality investments, or reinvest a portion of it back into growing the company further. In any event, it's fruitful to avoid going under the minimum amount you're committing monthly to your savings and investments. If you follow that practice, synchronous opportunities to generate or earn more emerge; the extra business comes in, although you may not know where or how. I may have a low week, and all of a sudden I'm on an airplane, I meet somebody who wants a business consultation, and another few thousand dollars synchronously emerges in order to fulfill my committed weekly savings amount. Initially I saved and then invested monthly, then every two weeks, and finally weekly to reduce the volatility in my business cash flow.

As I explained previously about negentropy and entropy, when you become organized and commit to automatically saving a guaranteed minimum amount or percentage (whichever is greater) up front into your savings, the money and business come to make sure that the minimum is covered. Putting that minimum amount in savings is almost like making a commitment decree to yourself and to the world.

Although many experts believe it is unwise to carry too much in a cash savings reserve, the top Fortune 100 companies generally have higher cash savings in reserve than other, less known companies. Warren Buffett's Berkshire Hathaway keeps over $100 billion in cash money market reserves or similar conservative, principal-preserving short-term CDs, T-bills, or bonds.

Spouses and Values

Respectful communication in marriage is a matter of communicating in terms of each other's higher values. Once I presented a relationship seminar program in Calgary, and there was a gentleman with a woman he was dating. He was a few years older. Both of them had been married before. He was a nice-looking, financially wealthy cattle rancher, probably worth about $11 million. She was very attractive and fun to be with, but she didn't have any money and had a little bit of debt.

The woman really wanted to marry the rancher. Whenever you have someone you really want, you're probably putting that individual a bit on a pedestal. That means she was minimizing herself and exaggerating him. She was pressuring him to get married, because she didn't want to lose this deal. People fear the loss of that which they are infatuated with or become emotionally attached to.

The rancher had recently gone through a divorce, so he was not so interested in immediately getting remarried—not with, as he called it, a "cost." He was resisting the idea of marriage; he just wanted some of the fringe benefits without the long-term commitment. The woman, on her side, was trying to leverage those fringe benefits into long-term commitment. It's the oldest exchange: beauty and sex for security and money.

The woman's urging was just alienating the man further. So I sat down and explained it to her: "Unless you communicate added value in terms of his highest values, you're not likely to get him to marry you. And as long as you think that he has something you don't, you're minimizing yourself relative to him. Why would he want to invest in somebody that's less than him? It's not a fair exchange."

So I had this woman write down where she had some hidden assets worth $11 million. "I don't," she said.

"As long as you don't, you're probably not going to marry him. Why would he want to invest in something and pay potentially half of his $11 million in the negotiation for that which is not perceived to be truly equal? Because that's what a marriage is: half of the property goes to the spouse. He's thinking, 'What's in it for me out of this deal?'"

At this point, you may be saying that this whole exchange is seemingly very commercial and transactional. Believe it or not, it is. When you go through a divorce, you realize that it really was all along—as little as you initially wanted to think about it that way. We want to be romantic, but the reality is, people are asking, "What's in it for me in this dynamic? What am I getting out of this deal? What am I receiving for what I am offering?" Men and women want the greatest package they can get for the offer they are bringing to the negotiation table.

They want someone who is preferably attractive and fit.

They want someone who is intelligent and creative.

They want someone who is ambitious and business-savvy.

They want someone who is resourceful and financially wealthy.

They want someone who loves, chooses, and desires them.

They want someone who is socially savvy and influential.

They want someone who is inspired, enthused, physically affectionate, loving, and grateful.

I sat with this woman for about an hour and a half and had her define and write down exactly how much value and worth she was contributing to her gentleman partner. I went around the wheel of life, which includes the seven primary areas of contribution: spiritual, mental, vocational, financial, familial, social, and physical. I helped her to see what she was bringing to the negotiation table in each of these areas and the dollar value of its worth to him. I helped her become consciously aware of what she was unconscious of in her contribution to their dynamic.

We started awakening her awareness of her greater worth and calculating it in terms of equivalent dollars—from her talents, skills, social connections, intelligence, and sexuality. I kept helping her become aware of her hidden assets. We kept totaling up the dollar value until it was equivalent to $11 million. She said, "Wow! I truly do have many hidden assets that I have been overlooking, and they are of great and equivalent value to my partner."

Then I said, "What do you think he has that you don't have?" Then I asked her where she displayed and demonstrated an equivalent in her life. What form was it in? Everybody is just a reflection of one another, so whatever the woman perceived in him, she had within herself in her own form. She had just not yet identified it. When she identified it, she immediately felt she was on the same playing field and was more confident.

Then I said, "If you're afraid of him leaving, did you have some fear in your past? Did somebody leave you?"

"Yeah, my ex-husband left me."

"So you're frightened that that's going to happen again. That's one of the reasons you want to hold on to him."

"Yeah."

"OK. What was the benefit of your ex-husband leaving you?" I helped her to neutralize the pain of that experience with benefits until we found the equal number of benefits in it. At that point, she no longer felt guilty or had a fear of loss. She stood her ground and said, "You know what? I'm a pretty decent catch."

"OK," I said. "Now you realize you have an equal value in the marketplace, so you don't desperately have to have him. Would you agree if you go into a club hoping to be attracting someone as a partner, if you go in there displaying desperate mannerisms, many men can sense it and stay away from you? When you don't enter with desperation and you feel confident and know you have a quality package to offer, men are drawn to you and approach."

I worked with this woman and helped her in elevating her self-image and self-worth. Her sense of urgency in having to have this man settled down. She felt more confident and selective.

While I was working with her, I also had the gentleman and the other attendees of the seminar complete the Demartini Method of conflict resolution, which is a method of dissolving emotional baggage over previous relationships. While I was helping her value herself and he was dissolving his past baggage, the man realized, "Oh my God, Dr. Demartini is now helping her empower her life, and she's now awakening more confidence and independence." Suddenly he was concerned that she might no longer want him. For the first time during their entire relationship, he started feeling less that he was in the "overdog" position. This leveled their playing field dynamic.

When lunchtime came, the man and woman walked up the main street downtown and spontaneously and mutually walked into a lovely jewelry store, and he bought her a $28,000 diamond engagement ring. Because she raised her self-worth and more effectively communicated value in terms of his highest values, she no longer exaggerated him and minimized herself. She saw what she was contributing to him. She no longer feared losing him. She came from a state of presence, identifying her own unique package of higher self-worth. The man, who had also balanced his perceptions, didn't want to lose that package, so he said, "I'm going to grab the opportunity to be with this woman."

In a few-hour period, the woman's situation went from "I am not getting married; I am not getting a ring" to "Here's my $28,000 ring." Of course, when we came back from lunch, every woman in the place surrounded her, checking out the ring and also looking at their boyfriends or husbands.

In short, marriage is a game of communicating in terms of each other's highest values. If you want your spouse to do what you would love, you can ask yourself, "What are their values? How do I communicate what I would love for them to do in terms of their highest values?" It's a matter of making them feel that it's their decision, because nobody makes decisions based on your values; they make it in terms of their own highest values. So you are to communicate what's most important to you in terms of what is most important to them.

If I want my wife to come to a program and I say, "Honey, I'm presenting a seminar program on quantum physics," is that going to make her come? It's unlikely.

But suppose I say, "Honey, I'm presenting a seminar program. It just happens to be at five-star hotel, which has a fabulous spa, where they have masseurs, pedicures, manicures, and fine shopping. And from what I hear, the masseur is a hunk. They have a shoe store in the building beneath and fabulous restaurants. I'll be off early in the afternoon from presenting at that seminar, and I thought that we might just walk hand in hand and stroll through the city, shop, go back and get you a massage, and maybe stop off at a jewelry store. I would love to have you join me if you would love to come to my seminar presentation." Is she more likely to come?

My late wife did the same respectful communication approach back to me. But before she learned the art of communicating in my values, she would just say, "I'd like you to take us out tonight to Le Cirque," which is a fine restaurant in New York.

My first response was generally, "A thousand bucks on an overly extravagant and rich dinner? Can't we just go to the sushi bar?"

Later, after she learned about communicating in terms of highest values, she would say, "I have a friend whose husband is the CEO of a large corporation, with 20,000 employees, and I heard from her that her husband is look-ing for an inspirational speaker. I just thought that maybe by going to dinner with them, you might use your skills of communication to close a deal, and it might be worth tens of thousands of dollars to you. I just thought that if you took us all to dinner, they might be able to help us in the future financially." Am I taking her to dinner? Of course.

If we help other people get where they want in life, we get where we want in life. The key is to care enough about another individual to communicate what's most import-ant to you in terms of what's most important to them. If you master the art of doing that, you can help them get to where they want, you can get to where you want to get, and you keep growing. This principle applies not only in rela-tionships at home, but in relationships at work, between you and the customer, with employees, and elsewhere. Remember, authenticity and sustainable fair exchange build income and ultimately financial wealth.

If you go to a sales course, you will learn that you are unlikely to sell the customer your products, services, or ideas until you find their dominant buying motive, or what they value most. Once you do, you communicate your product in terms of their motive, and you'll sell the product more easily. It's your responsibility as a salesperson to do that. Similarly, whenever you want your spouse or partner to do something, it's your responsibility, not theirs, to com-municate what you want in terms of their highest values.

9

Debt in Its Many Forms

et's talk about debt reduction. I can encourage you to write this down on a piece of paper:

Debt = previous investment in me

That's the definition: *previous investment in me*. Because if you owe people money, what does that mean? They obviously invested in you, believed in you, and trusted in you, and you now have the opportunity and responsibility to gratefully pay them back.

The first step is to reframe your thoughts on debt, much as you did with taxes. Debt by itself is neither good nor bad. Some forms of debt can be a great leveraging factor in investing when you are buying income-generating and appreciable assets, or they can seem to be a burden when you don't. You don't want to be angry at your debts or lenders, or they become harder to pay off. You want to be grateful for them, since they have contributed to your educational journey. People lent you some money; they believed in you. They took a risk by lending you their money. Since it represents a previous investment in you, debt is something to be grateful for. So write down the many benefits you have already received from your debt in order to be more inspired to pay it off.

The next step is to take your total debt. Let's say it's $100,000. Now you convert that into your monthly payment. How much is that payment per month over five years? It amounts to $1,667. Let's add in an estimated 5.3 percent interest, so that the figure comes to about $2,000 a month. Now break it down into weeks: dividing by 4 weeks, we get $500. Break it down further by 5 days a week: $100 a day. If we divide by 8 hours in a workday, we come down to $12.50 an hour. Now does a $100,000 debt seem more overwhelming than a simpler debt of $12.50 an hour? It gives a different psychological perspective. By breaking our financial objectives into bite-size actions steps, we make our financial wealth or freedom goal more easily obtained.

Another point: you have difficulty paying anything you don't want to pay. The lower it is on your value hierarchy, the more difficult it is to pay. You probably prefer not to pay for whatever's lowest on your value hierarchy; you love to pay whatever's highest.

This is why I've recommended that you actually appreciate your debt. Otherwise you'll have a hard time paying it, and you unconsciously will make it more difficult for you to pay off. If you appreciate it, you'll have an increased probability of paying it easily. So it's valuable to appreciate your debt. In some cases, debt leveraged wisely can be a great source of financial wealth, at least when you buy money-producing or appreciating assets with what you borrowed.

Next, you look at the cost of the primary service you provide. You take the number of clients you serve per day, and the average dollar that you earn per client—not gross, but net. You run your numbers, and you will probably find that it takes serving only one or two extra clients per day to pay your daily share of the debt.

If you're focusing on service, your debt goes away, because now you're focusing on the solution instead of the problem, on what will serve people instead of what was formerly perceived to be a financial weight on your back. If you focus on debt, your service goes away. It is wise to prioritize your focus.

In short, it's important to see your debt as an investment that has been made in you. Be grateful for it. Raise it on your appreciation list, so it's easy to pay. You tend to see opportunities for anything that's high on your value list. Then convert numbers down to a daily service, and focus on serving clients by that amount. Again, if you convert debt into service and focus on service, the debt goes away. If you're grateful for the debt, it's easier to make it disappear or use it to leverage even more income.

I also suggest that you write a thank-you letter for every check you pay: "Thank you for investing in me." This means that when the debt is paid, the creditor may want to invest again in case you ever choose to borrow and leverage again.

When I started my business, I borrowed some money. I am grateful a bank lender believed in me! He initially lent me $70,000 to open my practice; when I expanded my business, the financial market cycle had turned down, but he still lent me another $70,000, once I had a cosigner and provided some collateral. When I paid them off, which took two years, the bank was ready to give me more money if I wanted it. My track record of efficiently paying off my debt made me more creditworthy.

If you would love to borrow money from a bank for the first time, they'll probably want you to provide collateral nearly equal to the amount you're borrowing. If you don't have the collateral and can't show them something of value—a business plan, a history—that's going to give them the impression you're going to be able to pay the principal and interest in a timely manner, why would they give it to you? As soon as you can show them that you have a viable package equal in value to what they're going to lend you, they'll probably give you the money.

Remember the principle I mentioned previously: "How do I get handsomely or beautifully paid to do the next step of either starting or growing my business:" You just may be able to come up with an ingenious way to make money doing what you love more than borrowing money to do what you love. Sometimes preselling products, services, or ideas in advance is a way to generate income without borrowing.

Dealing with Discouragement

You're probably going to have an occasional moment when you're a bit discouraged and you're thinking, "Oh my gosh, I don't know if I'm going to make it." It's wiser to grin and bear it instead of robbing your savings or investments. I've had a few of those moments over the years when my business had a lull period. Once I had a lull for ten or twelve days. A bit of my reserve savings went out and the staff got paid, but some of the vendors didn't get paid immediately. I called or had my assistant call some of them and say, "There's going to be a little delay."

As long as you're communicating with your creditors and have every intention of paying, they tend to be very receptive and patient. But I didn't stop my automatic savings and investing because of the law of the lesser pissers, which jokingly says, *when you have a choice of pissing others off or pissing yourself off, always choose to piss others off.* Rising to the occasion and producing more income is wiser than falling to the occasion and rescuing yourself. Don't rob Peter to pay Paul. The next time this lull occurred, I became creative and figured out how to promote and generate more income instead of robbing my savings.

Loans and Lending

Let's say you owe money on a loan for your house. As you pay it off, you gradually and eventually have equity accumulated in the house that exceeds the amount that you owe. In this case, you may be using your mortgage as an indirect forced savings program. I believe that if many Americans didn't have mortgages to pay off, they'd probably have few or no appreciating assets when they retire, because of the lower value they have had in truly building financial wealth. But because the mortgage company can take their house back, they make the payments. We often pay for purchases by priority according to what will penalize us most if we did not pay.

That's why it's not the greatest idea to lend anybody money. You may have lent some money to a friend and then lost that friend. As Shakespeare writes, "Loan oft loses both itself and friend." I suggest that you consider not lending out your money, even to your family members; make them work for it, or have them go to a financial institution to borrow the money, one that holds them financially accountable. Don't rob people you love of dignity, accountability, responsibility, or productivity by possibly making them feel dependent or entitled.

My dad cosigned on the second business loan that I took out when I was expanding my practice. He said, "Let's go to the bank." I was paying 7.4 percent just to the bank. And then he said, "I will cosign some collateral for your loan, and I'm charging you an additional 4 percent for my collateral." He had all these criteria for his portion of tied-up capital, as well as a late fee, a penalty fee. I ended up paying almost 11.4 percent. Now did I want to pay 11.4 percent? Definitely not. My dad taught me that you only pay things back if the pain of not paying it is greater than the pain of paying it—and they know the penalty of not paying it back is high enough. That's where the Mafia comes into place. If you know that a loan shark will come over and rip your ear off as a reminder to pay him, you typically will pay because you want to keep your ears—even at a high interest rate.

If you ever think you want to lend money to anybody, I suggest that you take a shower, lie down, and relax until the desire goes away.

Here are the laws of lending: One is, don't. But let's say you're a so-called compassionate sucker and you end up doing it to compensate for conscious or unconscious guilty actions from your past, or for hidden agendas of your future. If so, it's prudent to write down an accountable payment schedule. Let's say the individual is borrowing $20,000. They are going to pay you back $500 twice a month for 24 months (to include the interest).

The payment schedule also requires a specific date: the first and the fifteenth of each month. Each payment is to be designated precisely as a specific amount; there also is a late fee, say a certain percentage of the total note per day, up to 1 percent a month. In addition, it's also wise to make sure the borrower has a steady income source that exceeds their normal bills, so they will be able to make this payment. This is what the bank does when you borrow money from it.

You would also be wise to ask for collateral: some asset, a car, a certain amount of stock. I would also recommend that the borrower read Napoleon Hill's *Think and Grow Rich,* George S. Clason's *Richest Man in Babylon,* or my earlier book *How to Make One Hell of a Profit and Still Get to Heaven* to inspire them to pay. I also suggest that you stipulate that they will be required to pay any legal fees if they deny payment.

If somebody comes to you and says, "I want to borrow some money" and you present that arrangement to them and they say anything other than thank you, they're telling you, "I'm not planning on paying you." If they react and say, "How dare you! I thought you were my friend," they have no intention of paying you. If you lend the money to them anyway, they will come up with excuse after excuse and constantly avoid paying you. You may have already lost friends this way.

If you don't have those safeguards in place, there's no guarantee that the borrower will repay you, unless the penalty of nonpayment is greater than the penalty of payment. One reason credit card interest rates are so high is that the companies know that if they aren't, people will just keep dragging out the payments.

Rescuing Desperation

A female acquaintance of mine once came to me asking for money. She had a low value on making or managing money or financial wealth building. Furthermore, her spouse did not produce or save much income; in fact he was more of a cost than an asset as far as income was concerned. She eventually divorced him, partly because of his low contribution levels, and then she returned to live with her family of origin.

For most of this woman's life, her father assisted or rescued her financially. She was taken care of. Some people might say that she was oversupported and protected and was not given many financial accountabilities or responsibilities.

In contrast, I had the opportunity to fend for myself and live on streets starting at age thirteen. I learned to take care of myself and how to be financially viable, and I became a young entrepreneur.

But this woman's father took care of, rescued, supported, and disabled her until she married, and he partly took care of her and her spouse from that time forward. One way or another, she would repeatedly get behind on paying her bills and debts, and her father would bail her out. When you bail people out financially and make it too easy on them, they often delay their growth and their appreciation for financial wealth building. That's why rescuing desperation is not wise. It means you're taking money from a more highly ordered, more disciplined state and putting it into a less ordered or more chaotic state. When you do, you dissipate money. It unwise to give money downhill, to less ordered systems—only uphill, to more ordered systems. Otherwise, your money will dissipate. Rescuing desperation backfires. It is wiser to educate, encourage, and invest in inspiration and help people to be financially accountable. Feed someone, and you feed them for a day. Teach them how to feed themselves and you feed them for a life.

In any case, this woman's father kept rescuing her and robbing her from productivity, accountability, responsibility, and dignity. When the father died, she received a moderate inheritance, and she lived on it temporarily for months until it ran out. She then accumulated $6,700 in debt. That was when she called me up and said, "I'm having

a problem. I just want to know if you can pay these bills."
She assumed I would take care of her because I have plenty
of money and possibly because I am about her father's age.

"What happened?" I asked.

"I've gotten myself in debt again, and I need to get out."

"Thank you, but no thank you; I care about you too
much."

This woman assumed I would bail her out, because
she'd been living off a financial umbilical cord. She was
intelligent in many areas, but not in finance or money
management. It was low on her value list. She was never
in an accountable position of learning how to manage it.
Anything that's low on your value list is where your chaos
is. Whatever is high on your value list is where your order
is. She had very high order in certain areas of her life, but
not in the area of making or wisely managing money.

I told her I wouldn't bail her out. At first she was
stunned when I did not live up to her fantasy. But she realized that the bailouts were now over, so she went out, got
two jobs, and got herself out of debt. She even started a
savings program. She later thanked me. She said, "It's the
first time in my life that I've had to figure out how to take
care of my bills all by myself."

"One of the greatest days of your life was when you
discovered you could take care of yourself, wasn't it?"

She goes, "Yes, it certainly was, I feel like now I'm able
to do it all on my own." She had been angry at her husband,
angry at her dad, angry at me. This was partly because she
eventually resented those upon whom she depended financially. She once unwisely believed that everybody was sup-

posed to take care of her. She's now saving her money and building some financial wealth. This woman had a major transformation, because now nobody has to rescue her.

Rescuing people can keep them stuck financially, and their response is commonly resentment. When you continue to rescue, they'll keep giving you new stories, and when you finally refuse, they'll resent you because you won't rescue them again. They will often use emotional blackmail and guilt trips to try to hook you again. You'll think, "But I helped you so much," At that moment, they are probably not focused on what you did in the past. They are resenting you because you are not doing it again and you previously added to their dependency.

It's not wise to rescue desperation. Invest in inspiration, and put money toward more highly ordered systems, where it is well managed. Either master the science of managing money well or give your money to people you trust who know how to manage it better than you. Money grows where it is organized and dissipates when it's put toward chaos. If you hand money to someone that doesn't know how to manage it, they're just going to go back to that same position again, like water seeking its own level.

If you value others more than yourself, you're going to spend your life rescuing people or sacrificing yourself. This leads to an unfair exchange, which will only provide you with a painful feedback lessons to return you to sustainable fair exchange. Actually, you're trying to a part of yourself that you haven't loved yet. If you see a fifteen-year-old that's so destitute that you want to rescue him, it's because there's a fifteen-year-old part of you that perceives itself as not being completely loved and appreciated. You rescue people on the outside that represent parts of you on the inside you have not loved—parts of you that are feeling obligated or guilty in regard to someone. You're rescuing a part of your old past. If you clear that aspect of yourself so it's not running your life, you can get on with valuing yourself, building financial wealth, and inspiring others.

Many so-called altruistic acts are compensations for shame and guilt of the past or hidden agendas of the future.

Paying Off Loans

Let's say you owe money for a mortgage or a car or furniture, and you want to pay that off. Here's my rule of thumb: do not rob your savings or stop your habit of savings and investments to pay off the loan. Instead, I suggest that you pay the loan while continuing to pay into savings, because I can almost guarantee you're going to pay off the loan, but I can't guarantee you'll repay your savings. Do both; accelerate both. Every quarter, it's a great idea to try to raise both by 5 or more percent. Push yourself. But it's not wise to rob Peter to pay Paul. Don't use your savings to pay off debts unless there is a drastic difference in interest rates. If there is, in some cases it may be wiser to get a secondary consolidated loan at a slightly lower rate or continue paying both while allocating a somewhat higher percentage toward the loan. But don't rob your habit of saving or your actual savings, because if you are paying off your note, the lender has the money. If you continue your savings, *you* have the money. Keep control of your principal.

I encourage you to continue to save and invest and still pay off the debt, even if the rate on the debt is 2 or more percent higher than on your savings, because having that liquid cash cushion is worth that 2 percent. I can almost guarantee you will pay that note off, but I can't always guarantee that you'll repay that withdrawal from your savings. When most people pay off their debts, they don't immediately convert that money into savings. Most of them will buy something else and get back into debt again. Or they'll raise their lifestyle without increasing savings and taxes by equal amounts and will delay the achievement of their goal of financial freedom.

I suggest that about thirty to sixty days before you know you're about to finish paying off your debt, you set up an automatic withdrawal to convert your previous debt payments into savings and investments. Otherwise, two things can occur. Your business income can drop by that amount, or you'll buy new depreciating items and return to having debt. This is sometimes due to a long-term history of living in and paying off debts instead of saving and then investing.

It is unwise to rescue yourself. It is wiser to find a way to serve more people and earn more income. If you start robbing your saved money, which you worked hard for, to immediately eliminate a debt just because you're under stress, you're right back where you started. Don't rob your savings. Care about and serve more people and earn more.

The meaningful and empowered attitude toward savings and then investments is that once it's saved, it's gone—untouchable. That's why there are penalties for early withdrawals from IRAs and 401(k)s: the government realizes that if you have access to your money too easily without a penalty and you use the money, you're starting over: you're losing time and the compound interest that you'd gained. As a result, it's preferable to have your money where it's not too easily accessible. Buy and hold it. Be a net buyer and let it compound and grow.

My advice is to initially live moderately within your means, automatically save and invest the difference, and be disciplined and committed over the long term. Only raise your lifestyle when you have earned the right.

Stores used to have layaway programs whereby you would buy an item, the store would hold it, you would make payments, and you would have the item once it was paid for. It's been reversed today. Immediate gratification has undermined discipline and long-term thinking, saving and investing.

Today people get credit cards. They don't pay for an item until after they own it. They're used to immediate gratification, so they get themselves into significant sums of debt on credit cards, because they think they've got something they don't.

There's power and leverage in paying for something in cash. A part of you says, "Hey, I've got that." There was a wisdom in the old saying, "Payment is due when services are rendered." Whenever you separate the pleasure of buying from the pain of paying, you activate the subcortical amygdala more than the frontal cortex and become more vulnerable to managing your money foolishly.

The Full Purse

There is another old saying that when thy purse is empty, more money exits thy purse; when thy purse is full, more money enters thy purse. I recommend that you apply this literally: carry whatever you want to make in a day as cash in your wallet or purse.

I have done that for years since I was twenty, progressively expanding the amount. Whatever I wanted to make in a day, I carried in cash. If I wanted to make $10,000 a day, I carried $10,000 with me. Eventually my income per day exceeded what I could easily carry. It climbed to over $30,000 a day. But carrying cash on me gave me a different feeling than being without it. It is like driving with a full tank of gas versus driving on empty. The former gave me a greater feeling of abundant confidence and the latter, a feeling of lack. I did not spend the money. It was simply seed money to draw in and crystallize chain reactions of financial opportunities.

People used to say, "Oh my God, that could be stolen." I didn't concern myself with that possibility. It was too insignificant; it was only a day's worth of income. If it was stolen, I figured I would replenish it. I didn't touch the money; it was just there as a catalyst. But I carried whatever I wanted to make in a day. Psychologically, it was an affirmation. And it more than paid off.

Have you ever seen wealthy people that carry a big wad of money? Up until the digital age, this was more common, but it still occurs today. I started to notice that the wealthiest of my patients often had a roll of money, and they paid in cash. So I carried money with me—in the largest denominations I could find, $100 bills, so it didn't overbulk—but I carried it. Since I have done that, the amount that I began generating has become greater than the amount carried and much more than the loss of interest on what I could be earning on it. There was a psychological benefit, because I walked, talked, thought, and acted differently when I had cash in my pocket.

10

Marriage and Family

If you are the primary breadwinner in your family, my advice is, do not assume that the money is all yours. I have mediated divorces on many occasions and have helped the partners both restructure their finances. In one case, the man was making $250,000 a year and the wife was making $20,000 a year. Because she earned a smaller portion of their income, the husband assumed that all the money was his, and he didn't want to lose any of it in the divorce process.

"Excuse me," I said to him, "that money you have—it's not all yours."

"What do you mean, it's not mine? I worked hard for this."

"No," I said, "that's not how it works. Half of it is hers. When you signed the marriage contract, you declared she was half owner—unless of course you had a prenuptial arrangement."

"So she's trying to get what's hers? But that's not fair. I was the one who worked and earned it." He didn't think that her raising of his three kids was work. Of course that was his delusion. And he forgot what financial responsibilities he signed up for when he got married.

To deal with this possibility, there are prenuptial agreements and now divorce insurance in the United States. If you're divorced, you get to keep your assets; the insurance policy pays your spouse's half.

The insurance companies have questionnaires to compute these probabilities in advance. They ask questions that get through to your subconscious to find out, for example, what your home, family, and sex life is like. Company representatives come out and evaluate your marriage. The insurance companies have actuarial tables to compute the odds, and they'll charge significant premiums based on the likelihood of a couple divorcing within one, five, or ten years. One gentleman claimed to have it down to an 87 percent probability whether a given couple was going to divorce.

If you're married and you are the breadwinner, I recommend that you earmark half of your money as not yours. Psychologically, you need to keep that in your mind, because if you don't, you could start to exaggerate your and minimize your spouse's financial and other contributions.

Salaries for Spouses

A further approach: suppose that one spouse is the breadwinner and the other is the homemaker. (Either role could be taken by either partner.) Take the spouse who's caring for the family instead of doing a job out there making "income." Figure out whatever it would cost at fair market value to replace every single duty they do, including nurturing and educating the children, maintaining the home, shopping, cooking, lovemaking, and so on, and pay the homemaker that amount. (After all, if they died, you'd have to pay money to have someone perform all those tasks.) This amount is the spouse's salary, and out of that, they pay their share of the bills, with some additional and respectful spending money left over. That way, in case of a divorce, you'll be able to find out the partners' real contributions instead of basing their claims on the emotions of what they think they own. Some spouses, once they realize all of the responsibilities their partners are managing, become deeply humbled and realize they could hardly afford all of their spouse's replacement costs if they had to pay them all upon divorce.

By failing to think this through in a caring, honest, objective, and open manner, you could gradually isolate the breadwinner and their income from the one who's not directly making the money while making it possible for the breadwinner to do so. One spouse could devalue themselves in the market, the other will exaggerate themselves, and the partners can become alienated and distant.

But if each spouse is being paid fairly for their many services, the couple is dividing the assets at the beginning. Neither partner devalues or exaggerates themselves. This keeps more of an even keel, and the couple grows together. If you're married, I recommend doing that. It makes a huge difference. It reduces the distortion and makes the dynamic more objective.

Relationships can deteriorate because each partner mirrors the other. It's a matter of discovering your own highest values, discovering your mate's highest values, and mastering the art of communicating your highest values in terms of theirs, so you have communication with dialogue instead of alternating monologue.

It's also helpful to establish and periodically reestablish goals and visions that you have in common, as well as visions that you have separately, because there's health in having both. It's unproductive to have to sacrifice your life for them or have them sacrifice their life for you. Every human being wants to be loved for who they are, not who they're supposed to be according to some fantasy being projected.

Another part of maintaining a financially viable relationship is knowing how to dissolve baggage from previous relationships that you're carrying into this one.

Sometimes people get married in an infatuation phase. You may have been infatuated with somebody: you couldn't get them out of your mind; you lay in bed and fantasized; you couldn't even work because you were mentally preoccupied. You may also have stopped focusing on some of your own dreams. You started minimizing yourself for the other: whenever you infatuate and put people on pedestals, you minimize yourself in relation to them. You inject their values into your life, exaggerate them, and try to live according to their life instead of your own. You'll eventually resent the other partner because you're not feeling loved for who you are; you're feeling loved only if you're living their life. When you repress your own highest values in order to fit into theirs, you eventually build up resentments until your repression explodes.

Then you'll go to the other side. Instead of putting your beloved on a pedestal, you'll put them in the pit. At first, you'll be blinded by infatuation, then you'll be blinded by resentment, because true love perceives both sides simultaneously, but infatuation and resentment are polarized and blind. When you're resentful, you're seeing negatives without positives, and when you're infatuated, you're seeing positives without negatives. Yet nobody has one without the other; they inevitably have a pair of opposites. True love consists of both what I admire and despise in the beloved: attraction and repulsion. Even lovemaking is built out of the mechanics of both.

If you put your mate onto a pedestal of infatuation and decide to get married impulsively and spontaneously, you will get distracted from your more objective reason. You want to have your heart and your mind working together, so it's wise to stop and reflect: does this individual really have what I'm looking for in each of the seven areas of life? True reasoning will not close the heart. True reasoning will only reopen the heart. If you are expecting a one-sided partner, you will become broadsided by the side you overlooked or ignored.

This topic is included in this book because many individuals who start down the road of accumulating financial wealth can have their total net worth become divided on one or more occasions. This is because they have not had sufficient foresight and reason to learn how to respectfully communicate respectfully. Sustainable fair exchange, even with your spouse, is one key to lasting financial freedom.

Seven Areas of Compatibility

As implied previously, when you're considering marriage, it's helpful to do some analysis and look at your potential mate in respect to the seven areas of life: spiritual, mental, vocational, financial, familial, social, and physical. You might even think in terms of a scale from 1 to 10.

On the spiritual level, you can ask, is your potential mate an awakened, inspired self-actualized being? Are they spiritually empowered? Where would you put them on a scale of 1 to 10?

Then you can look at your mate and see where they are mentally or intellectually. It might not necessarily be a matter of formal education; some people are not highly educated but have remarkable creativity and intuition.

You can also look at their vocation or career. Does your mate have an inspiring and meaningful career? Are they empowered, skilled, and accomplished in that career? Do they have influence in their profession?

Then you can look at your potential spouse from a financial perspective. Do they have some capacity for wise financial management? Do they know how to build and manage financial wealth? Do they have their own income, savings and investments?

Next comes family. Is your partner appreciative, caring, loving and emotionally stable? Do they communicate well? Are they likely to be there for you in the inevitable times of difficulty?

You are also wise to look at your potential mate from a social perspective. Do they have social power and influence? Are they well connected? Are they socially contributing and making some difference?

Finally, there is the physical aspect. Where is your mate on the physical scale? Are they fit, attractive, and wellness-conscious? Do they respect their physical well-being? Do you find them beautiful or handsome and sexually attractive? That's a part of the picture, even if it's only a part.

Believe it or not, in a relationship, everybody's asking, "What's in it for me?" as well as "What is the full package I am offering?" As much as we like to think it's all romantic all the time, it comes down to what's in it for me? Am I getting what I want out of this deal? Remember, sustainable fair exchanges underlie stable and lasting relationship dynamics.

Then it's wise to look at your mate in respect to yourself. Let's say that you are a male, and you consider your female mate a 9, factoring in all seven areas of life. If you don't believe you're a 10 and perceive yourself to be a 7, you are going to be wanting to hold on to your partner and not lose her, because you will be in the underdog position in the relationship. If you perceive her to be a 6 and you feel you are an 8, you are going to say to her, "Not yet—get your seven areas of your life together first." You will then be in the top dog position in the relationship.

But if you have got a partner who's on the same level overall, a match, and one who can banter with you, you have a higher probability of having a more stable relationship. Even though you may have one area stronger, your partner may have another area stronger. A relationship is more likely to be sustainable when the overall level is similar, where there is equity. Otherwise, one partner is up and the other one is down, or vice versa. This results in narcissistic and altruistic behaviors, almost like parent and child dynamics.

I've seen this happen. There may be an attractive woman who has little to no income, like the woman in Calgary whom I mentioned previously. She was involved with a man that had quite a bit going for him. She didn't believe she offered much initially until I reawakened her self-image and her unconsciously stored power.

We all have hidden power, but we don't always wake up to it. If you don't, you don't demonstrate it. If you don't demonstrate it, you may perceive a difference. Once this woman woke up and raised her bar high enough, the man said, "This is a greater catch than I first recognized." As long as she was minimizing herself and looking up to him, he wasn't interested. He was the top dog, and she was the underdog, but only because of her perceptions.

If you're going to get married, it's wise to find out where your mate is in relation to the seven areas of power. Do they really have power there? Be honest about them and yourself.

Once a daughter of a client said, "I'd love to marry a confident, wealthy man."

"What are you going to offer him in return?" I said. "Did you think your looks alone are going to do it? You currently have beautiful looks, but it is unwise to rely only on your looks. That temporary asset alone won't necessarily guarantee that the relationship is going to hold. It can eventually depreciate in value. Make sure that you have something else to contribute."

You may want to be able to contribute to your spouse socially. You may want her to be able to say, "Hey, that's my husband" with a feeling of high value. If you won't want to say, "This is my wife" or "This is my husband" in front of people, you know you have some blockage and devaluation occurring.

It's wise to empower all seven areas of your life and have goals to contribute in all of them. If you do, you increase your odds in the marketplace. There is no lack of opportunity in the marketplace for a high-quality and high-standard package. To view a relationship from an economic perspective (since money is simply a means of exchanging one value for another), the more valuable you are, in each of the seven areas of life, the more money you have the potential to receive, because the more you can contribute to people's lives. It's not unwise to grow both in your self-worth and your net worth.

When it comes to managing money, it's wise for each spouse to have their own individual incomes, savings, and investments as well as common savings or investments for objectives that both parties have in common. It's valuable for your partner to have the freedom to do whatever they want with some portion of their money. You would love to have that, because you would love that same freedom in my life. Of course, you also love having the opportunity to enjoy activities together.

When two partners have a respectful and sustainable fair exchange going on financially their combined contribution to their overall financial wealth building is enhanced.

Children

As for raising children relative to money, my advice is to give them daily or weekly chores or responsibilities for which they are accountable. Make them work for what they receive—in other words, get them used to the realities of life. I was blessed to have a father who helped me in this way. I approached him when I was age nine and told him I wanted to buy a baseball, glove, and bat. He said, "Son, if you want these items, you will be required to earn the money to buy them. If you want to do that, you can do plenty of things around the house over and above your normal chores to earn extra money."

Every Sunday, I had the opportunity to shine my dad's, mom's, sister's, and my shoes before we all went to church. I'd shine four pairs, and I got a dollar. That was decent money in those days.

Here is what my mom also did: Starting when I was age two, she used to walk me to the store with her. She showed me how to look both ways before walking across the very busy street. By age four, she had taught me how to go to the grocery store, which was about a quarter of a mile away, on my own and count and exchange money. Then it became my responsibility to buy some of the weekly groceries. She gave me exactly the amount of money needed for the groceries, plus a nickel for a Baby Ruth candy bar.

If I got all the groceries that she wanted and brought them home safely, I got to eat my candy bar. Of course she would call the store in advance and say, "My son will be there in the next eight to ten minutes. If he's not, let me know." If I didn't want to buy the candy bar, I could keep the nickel. I could accumulate some nickels that way and save for something more valuable. I often deferred my immediate gratification for something more valuable.

I also had a little paper route, which I didn't love doing as much after a while, so I dumped it; I felt it was too much work for the small amount I was earning. Then I went into doing yardwork, clipping hedges and sweeping and raking in the fall. I did anything I could around the neighborhood, because my dad said, "You can have anything you want, but you will be required to earn it. So you will be required to look for home or neighborhood opportunities to earn money as often as you would love to earn. The more opportunities you can find, the more money you can earn."

By age nine, I knew how to effectively and efficiently do everything about yard maintenance. I also went with my dad to his business. He had a plumbing business, so I cleaned out pipes with a brush. For every 200 nipple or couple pipes I brushed and oiled, I received a dollar.

When I was nine, I earned enough money to buy a bicycle. It was the coolest thing, because everybody else in the neighborhood had their parents buy them a bicycle. But my dad made me earn the money to buy it. He didn't give me something for nothing, which I appreciate. He was giving me freedom, teaching me how to have independence and how sustainable fair exchange works. There was no limit on what I could earn if I was willing to be unlimited with my service.

My dad also taught me how to ask for what I want. He'd tell me, "Go up to that house, knock on the door, and ask if they have some chore or landscaping activity that you can do to earn money." It's amazing how many kids on the street wouldn't do that. The parents on the street told me, "You can take the trash out, and I'll give you a quarter." "You can gather all the leaves on the yard, and I'll give you $2." "You can clean off all the cobwebs on our windows and make $2." I went around the neighborhood, trying to find things to do, and I learned how to get what I wanted by helping others get what they wanted. Today it's very common for kids to expect to just be given what they want. I am grateful my parents made me more financially accountable.

All of these lessons gave me a work ethic. I've found that people who have a work ethic go much farther financially than people that don't. Those who really want something out of life will be willing to do whatever it takes within reason to get it. I have as an affirmation: *I'll do whatever it takes, travel whatever distance, and pay whatever price to give my service of love across the world.*

I also believe that it is wise for children to learn how to save by starting out with piggy banks. If you learn the habit of saving, a piggy bank becomes a biggy bank. When I was a kid, I used to count my money—all the pennies, nickels, dimes, quarters, fifty cent pieces, silver dollars, and notes. I looked to see if there were some old, rarer coins, because I knew those were more valuable than their face value.

I'm stressing the importance of teaching your children that you don't get something for nothing: people generally get what they pay for. There is certainly an abundance of opportunities to make a great income and living, so look for those opportunities: they're certainly around you. Care about serving humanity, and abundance is yours. I don't believe there's such a thing as someone who can't find a job. The only one that can't find a job is someone who's not really looking.

The Crystal Cathedral

In the winter of 1976, I had the opportunity to meet with the late inspirational minister Robert Schuller. He told me that he was being criticized for considering building his large Crystal Cathedral, an eighteen-million-dollar project in Garden Grove, California. He said he was frightened at times and didn't know how he was going to do it, but he felt this was his inspiration. He said, "I'm destined to do this, and if I'm destined to do it, I'll work twenty-four hours a day, and I'll inspire people to help me do it."

At the time, Schuller was attacked by thousands of people for spending money on that project instead of feeding the poor.

But he said, "I'm building this to inspire my churchgoers and TV viewers to do what's possible inside their lives—to show them that inside them is an idea that is so inspiring to them that they can bring it into this world and actually manifest it and inspire other people to participate in it. Otherwise we're rescuing desperation and supporting people in what they can't do instead of encouraging and inspiring people in what's possible."

Schuller built his Crystal Cathedral in Garden Grove, California from 1977 to 1981. He commissioned the world-famous architect Philip Johnson to design it, and when it was completed, it contained 10,000 rectangular pieces of glass. It was finished in 1981, and a prayer spire was added in 1990. At the end of Schuller's life, his organization fell into financial difficulties, and finally the cathedral was sold to the local Catholic diocese, but it still remains as a magnificent achievement.

Those with an inspiring purpose are quite often attacked; it's part of the game. To be great is to be misunderstood. Whenever somebody contributes something new, it's automatically going to be challenged by people who can't see the value and purpose of the vision.

In fact, it's valuable to be challenged along the journey. I've been attacked quite often. Once on television, I said, "It is not what happens to you that matters as much as how you perceive it and what actions you decide to take as a result of it. You can become a master of your destiny and not remain a victim of your history. It is your choice."

That angered many viewers, who preferred to blame others and give excuses for their misfortunes. At one point, I was written and verbally attacked by 8,000 people from a church who said I was the Antichrist because on television I had said, "No matter what happens to you, it's on the way and not in the way. There is a hidden order in your apparent chaos" They thought I was the Devil to say something like that. It just so happened that at that same moment I was being honored by 8,000 attendees at a convention in Las Vegas for being Chiropractor of the Year.

While you are building your financial wealth, you will be required to embrace both supporting and challenging events and people along the way. It is wise to use both sides as means to your end.

Embracing the challenges is part of the game of building financial wealth. It's not wise to let any so-called perceived obstacles interfere with your financial objectives and dreams. If you have a dream, let nothing stop you from that dream. If you want to be a wealthy, let nothing stop you—not even your own emotions, not even your own temporary distracting passions or impulses. Let there be no turning back.

11

Obstacles to Your Dreams

Let's look at factors that could interfere with achieving or fulfilling your financial dreams. One is death: you could die before you attain your goals. Other factors: disease, divorce, disability, inflation, taxes, speculative investments; business malpractice. Liability is another: somebody comes to your house, slips, falls, sues you, and wipes out your life's savings or nest egg of investments.

Longevity can also interfere with your dreams. Say you planned your finances expecting that you would live to age ninety, but you live to 100 (which is increasingly frequent these days). You may have already wiped out your principal, with another ten years to live.

Of course, there are many forms of protection, notably insurance: Life insurance, which is really death insurance. There's disease insurance, known as health insurance.

Some forms of insurance—such as cancer insurance—are intended to protect you against catastrophic illness. But in the United States, the insurer won't pay you unless you get treatment, although the treatment itself can also create side effects and kill you. A recent study at Johns Hopkins University concluded that iatrogenic disease—disease caused by medical care or treatment—is the third leading cause of accidental death in the United States. One of the main killers in this country is medical errors and pharmaceutical side effects.

It is wise to prevent illness by living according to sound wellness behaviors and valuing your physical existence. The longer you are alive, the longer you get to take advantage of the power of compound interest in helping you build financial wealth and freedom.

Inflation, Catastophic, and Disability Insurance

What's inflation insurance? Having a well-thought-out strategy for investing to make sure that inflation is not eating away at your accumulation of assets. Inflation in the U.S. has varied over the decades, but over the last 100 years it has averaged around 3–4 percent per year. As a result, the cost of living has doubled about every eighteen to twenty years. It's wise to plan on that continuing. Investing in quality assets with true intrinsic value can offset inflation.

When buying insurance, you want to get the highest-quality, stablest insurance company you can and negotiate the greatest possible deal for the greatest package. At first the premium payments may seem like a lot of money, but after a while, just like anything else, you may no longer notice them, and the cost is generally pretty stable; it generally doesn't go up once you've packaged it.

Of course, there are many other forms of insurance protection—such as catastrophic illness insurance—which is intended to protect you against cancer or heart attacks. But in the United States, the insurer won't pay you unless you get treatment, although the treatment itself can also create side effects and even kill you.

When my dad was around fifty-two, he got an updated disability insurance package. I think it was going to pay him $7,000 or $8,000 a month until he was sixty-five. He paid on it for four years. Then he and I were outside throwing sticks at the pecan trees (we had a pecan orchard). My dad twisted himself, his whole body went into spasms, and he fell on the ground. Fortunately, a doctor lived next door. I ran to get him, and he came over and gave my father an injection to calm his spasms down. We couldn't figure out what happened, but somehow it affected his spinal cord and brain.

A few months later, my dad started to show other symptoms. At first, his general medical practitioner didn't know what was going on. Finally, a doctor at the Diagnostic Clinic of Houston, saw my dad walking and said, "By the way, did you know you have Parkinson's disease?" This doctor did additional tests and found that indeed my father had Parkinson's. His condition deteriorated over the next few years, and he ended up receiving disability. In the end, I think he paid in for a total of seven years in and then started receiving $7,000–$8,000 a month back. He had paid in about $40,000 and got $350,000 back. Now I'm not saying for certain that you could have a disability; I'm just saying that in his particular situation, that was an extremely decent investment.

My parents lived in the country, and across the field from us was a 1,000-acre cotton field. Every year they would spray defoliants to remove the leaves from the cotton so they could pick it clean with machines.

When they sprayed the defoliant, they'd go right over my parent's and nearby neighbor's house, and the defoliant, laden with heavy metals and toxic chemicals, would land on the whole neighborhood. I think eleven out of nineteen neighbors had neurological diseases from the defoliant spray within a decade. My mom had Lou Gehrig's, my dad had Parkinson's, and the guy next door had a neuromuscular disease. Many of their neighbors had neuromuscular disease. They couldn't do anything about it legally, because the owner sold the land and died. It was just part of the challenges and risks of life.

My mother didn't have disability insurance, but my father had saved and invested, so she ended up having enough money to cover her costs the rest of her life. She lived till she was nearly eighty-two.

At age fifty, there's was a slim chance that my parents would have ever imagined that happening. You can't always foresee these situations. Right now, you may not be able to imagine yourself in those situations either, but there is a certain statistical probability that such illnesses could happen. Disability insurance can be of real value depending on the probability.

You can relinquish insurance if you get to a point where you have so much money actively or passively coming in and accumulated that it is no longer necessary. Insurance is not absolutely necessary if you feel you've got enough cushion, but if you don't, you might be wise to pay for the insurance. The same is true for life insurance. You can pay a minimal amount for term insurance until you have accumulated enough assets to pay off your mortgage and other probable life expenses.

Insurance and Inheritance

Life insurance is not mainly for you. It's mainly for the people that you pass your torch to: your children and your other survivors. I don't necessarily recommend giving all your money to your children, because if they don't know how to earn it or manage it, they can end up squandering it and becoming spoiled. I've seen people pass all their wealth to their kids, and the kids didn't work: they had no incentive or drive. In these cases, all the financial wealth is very commonly gone within two generations or even less. Rags to riches to rags. Tough times make strong people, Strong people make life easier. Easy times make weak people. Weak people make times tough. And the cycle begins again.

I once watched a television show about an extremely wealthy man in England. The interviewer asked him, "You have so much money. How do you treat your children? Do they work? Do they not work?"

"Of course they work. My children started in my company at minimum wage, and they had to work and earn every penny. And unless they saved a portion of their own income, they were not given promotions or new opportunities. So they had a strong drive to work, save, and invest. I did not treat them any differently than anybody else; they were not privileged, because that would undermine the respect they would receive from the rest of the people in the company. When they matured, they learned to appreciate not being given a special deal. They worked their way up and learned every different component of the company."

The interviewer asked, "You have billions of dollars. Are you going to leave your fortune to your children?"

"Absolutely not. Not unless they save, invest, grow, and manage their fortunes in a manner that they are worthy of such additional fortunes. And I will only leave an amount in their trust in proportion to how much they have served, saved, and invested, because that's all they've earned and know how to manage wisely. And they will rise to their own level of worth."

If you give people money that they have not earned and don't know how to manage, they can mismanage it and end up going back down to their true level of self-worth. If you rescue desperation instead of investing in inspiration, you can rapidly dissipate great fortunes. In that case, just say goodbye to your money.

It is not necessarily wise to give your money to your children just because they're your children; you give it to them because they've earned the right to manage and grow it. If not, give it to somebody who does know how: put it into a trust with qualified executors or trustees until the children have proved they can manage that level of money. When they have, they can become eligible to take it over; then they have the responsibility to pass that torch to the next generation. In this way, you can build a legitimate dynasty; you can build perpetuity.

12

The Power of Appearance

When I went to professional school, I was the only man to wear a dress shirt, tie, and jacket every day. Some people thought, "That's kind of weird. Why would you want to do that? You don't need to. You're just a student."

But I had a teacher whom I respected. He said, "If you don't practice being the doctor you desire to be now, you're going to have to get used to it later. So start now. The sooner you start, the more you're ahead. Dress like one, talk like one, act like one; *be* the doctor." Nobody else listened to him, but for some reason it made sense to me, and I decided to do it.

I didn't yet have a lot of money; all I had at first was a cheap little clip-on tie, a few cheap little Qiana dress shirts, some decent slacks, and a couple of dress jackets. Finally I bought a suit from J.C. Penney. It was reversible, with a houndstooth pattern on the outside and a solid on the inside. It was less than $160—not much of a suit, but it was the suit I could afford.

Looking back, I can see that out of all the people in my professional school class, I've made the most income and possibly had the most influence. I know that the many opportunities I have received had something to do with the way I presented myself.

One time when I was starting in my clinical practice, I was standing in line at a Kroger supermarket. I'd just been jogging, and I had a little blue and white jogging outfit on. I was standing there about to pay for some yogurt. One of my patients was in the same line ahead of me and suddenly saw me and said, "Oh, hi, Dr. Demartini." She could only see my face; she couldn't see what I was dressed in. She had a friend with her. She was waiting, and I came up to them. All of a sudden, she saw that I was just in my shorts and jogging T-shirt. She turned away, ignored me, and then walked off with her friend.

I thought, "She really wanted to introduce me to her friend, a possible new patient, but because of my presentation, she was feeling awkward and embarrassed. She avoided any further conversation and walked away." So I realized the impact and become even more accountable to dress professionally regardless of where I was for the sake of my patients and my career. After that, I noticed that people treated me noticeably more respectfully when I dressed more professionally.

Once I did a seminar in Houston and asked my daughter to help me. She came in an outfit that did not quite match what I thought would resonate with the seminar and attendees. Maybe she wasn't thinking or didn't know the significance of her attire, or maybe she was strategizing, figuring that Dad would buy her an outfit because she dressed that way. In any case, I went out with her and bought her an outfit I sensed would be more resonant with the setting. When she came to the program, she acted more professionally, and the people treated her differently.

Afterwards, we went to dinner, and my daughter said, "That was an amazing educational experience."

"What do you mean?"

"I was amazed at how people treated me."

"That's because the way you present yourself and dress has an impact on the way people perceive and treat you, what they expect, and what they're willing to invest time and money in."

I believe that when it comes to attire, quality is far more important than quantity. If you spend X dollars on clothes but buy cheap clothes, they won't make you feel like a million bucks. With high-quality clothes, even if you have to wear them over and over, you feel like a million bucks. I'd rather wear out my high-quality clothes and buy more again next year than have mere quantity. That does not necessarily mean buying the most expensive and often overpriced brands. It simply means that being dressed professionally opens up more doors professionally.

I once attended a seminar salon presented by Robert Panté that gave you a reality check on how you're presenting yourself. After going to this salon, I upgraded my wardrobe another notch. I said, "If I am going to be a multimillionaire, I'm going to start moving in the direction of one." I threw out every piece of clothing that didn't make me feel like a million bucks. I bagged it all and gave it away to Goodwill. Then I gradually filled my wardrobe item by item with higher-quality, more professional clothing—the highest I felt I could afford and find.

The very week I began doing this, I was asked to do an ongoing TV series. I also started receiving more speaking presentations to groups, because now I felt even more presentable. I hadn't even realized that I was holding myself back from some of my own goals. My speaking and media opportunities, and my income, moved up a notch.

For about the first week, I had a bit of a cash flow crunch, because I'd spent a bit more temporarily on upgrading my presentation. But weeks later, there was a noticeable acceleration of opportunity and income.

There's no doubt in my mind that the way you present yourself can make a difference in your business opportunities and income. You want to dress the part, but you want to dress in quality for that part. If you are selling horse equipment, you don't want to wear an Armani suit; you want to wear a fine cowboy outfit. You don't have to wear overly fancy clothes, but you want to wear quality for whatever matches your industry. It's valuable for a woman to dress in a nice outfit or suit to sell fabulous furniture. She couldn't possibly go in dressed too casually. She's wise to dress the part that matches the furniture. If she does, she may spend a little bit more, but she will make even more back in sales commissions. If you're an aerobics instructor, you want to have as nice an outfit as possible: clean, fresh, new, cutting-edge outfits. You don't want to be going in with ragged old clothes.

Of course, every time you raise your lifestyle, raise your savings, investing, and tax payments to help you attract more income or money to manage.

You can save money by timing your shopping expenses and taking advantage of sales. I buy suits from many places around the world. I know when they have sales on, and if I happen to be able to catch them, great.

You might as well talk to yourself this way: "I'm worth investing in. I'm a wealthy individual. I deserve the greatest, finest, most privileged life on this planet, but I am patient and will gradually earn the income, save, and then invest until my passive income allows me the right to have the life I would love."

Would you agree that surrounding yourself with the finest that life can offer can be inspiring? Not just for the sake of keeping up with or showing off to the Joneses, but for the sake of investing in quality creations and masterpieces and to help reward the masters who created them, thereby raising the overall social standards. You go to an art museum and you see some of the finest art; it inspires you. You see the world's greatest architecture, and it inspires you. It's wise to surround yourself with people that inspire you and invest in yourself to the point where you live a life that inspires both you and other people.

As Albert Einstein once stated, the greatest teacher is exemplification. Living an inspired life inspires others and gives them permission to do the same. Both of these draw economic rewards to you.

13

Charitable Giving

Have you ever been approached by somebody asking for a charity donation? They give you this spiel, and it's really moving. They say, "Would you love to donate to our cause?"

You say, "Yes, I'd love to donate $1,000, or any greater amount."

Then what happens? A year later, they're back again. When somebody comes back again and again for a donation, have you ever had the feeling that it seems to become more like an obligation than an inspiration? You give them another thousand, or more, but part of you starts thinking, "Next year, if they call, I think I'm going to be out of the office." Once it's an expectation, it's no longer an inspiration. It can go all the way down the imperative ladder from "want to" to "need to" to "ought to" to "have to": "Oh yeah, I've got to do it again; it's that time of year, I guess."

If you receive credit for giving initially, you can receive blame later if you don't. You run into the credit and blame cycle. You're a nice guy as long as you give, but they're irritated with you if you don't. There's a kind of rejection. It can work in your favor in the beginning, but it can work in your disfavor in the end. (Unless of course the cause still truly inspires you.)

Here's one possible recommendation: if a charitable cause comes along that inspires you, one way to keeping the giving inspiring is by doing it anonymously. You say to the individual who's soliciting, "Thank you, but no thank you." If you really feel inspired, figure out a way to put some cash in an envelope and have it secretly delivered to the location of the charity, where there's no way they can trace it. Then you don't tell one soul—your spouse, anybody. It's gone. It's an anonymous donation that nobody on this planet ever knows about but you.

Now you're not necessarily going to get a tax advantage this way (because that would reveal who is giving and to what). You keep it a secret. Nobody knows about it. If someone comes next year to ask for a donation, again say, "Thank you but no, thank you." If you tell somebody about your gift, you dissipate its power. If you don't, you have this secret charitable effect. I can't explain it, but it's worth the money, however much you give. It's a certain inner, secret, vibrational energy impact.

If you're going to give to some charity, I also suggest that you investigate whom you're giving it to beforehand. I learned this from the Rockefellers. They had so many charities that they learned what to do and what not to do. They have a fantastic textbook on charities, and they have rules of charitable contribution.

First, don't give to a charity unless the individual who's managing its money knows how to manage it wisely and the money is producing more than it is costing. That means the assets that you provide will accelerate and grow, which in the long run will allow you to make a longer, more impactful contribution.

In many charities, only 4.7 percent of the money you give actually has to go to the actual advertised cause: if you give them $1,000, only $47 may go that year to the actual cause. It's because they have the right to put the rest of the funds into an asset base for investing to keep the charity going. They're only authorized to give about 5 percent of that money to the intended outcome that year, minus some costs. If they invest the rest where it appreciates, the money you gave is going into an asset base that keeps giving back to the actual cause, which means over time you are actually going to be contributing more over time than your original amount. The Rockefellers knew that, so they did not invest in a charity unless they knew that its foundation base of money was appreciating in value and meeting a worthy need.

If you are giving to a charity to publicize yourself or your company, don't call it a charitable contribution. Call it a fair exchange marketing cost. You're thinking that by giving, it'll put you on a list; it'll open some doors; it'll get you some business; you're hopefully going to get some return out of it. If you find that after years you're not getting more than you're giving, you will probably stop. That's because your incentive was marketing. So just call it a marketing cost; this just happens to be your marketing outlet.

There are some other factors that are important to be aware of if you're giving to a charity. It's wise to make sure that whatever that money's going to is not robbing people of four things: dignity, accountability, responsibility, and productivity. Otherwise, you may be giving money to perpetuate the problem you're trying to solve.

Generally speaking, fertility rates drop when educational levels increase. If you feed people without educating them, they can keep multiplying at a rate such that you'll actually have more mouths to feed.

One lady with a Christian organization that fed children in Africa came to one of my seminars in Canada, and she said, "Oh, my God, you're right. I have four children that I've been feeding for eight years, since they were six years old. They're all fourteen years old, and a couple of them are now pregnant." This means that they possibly won't be able to complete an education: they'll be focused on their children. If you give money to feed people but don't educate them, it's possibly robbing them of dignity, accountability, productivity, and responsibility.

If you give money to a charitable organization that feeds people, it's wise to make sure that the organization is combined with an educational organization. That reduces the probability that the beneficiaries will be robbed of dignity, accountability, responsibility, and productivity; then they have a chance to grow and be self-sufficient. Whenever you invest in somebody in a way that keeps them from being self-sufficient, you're dissipating your money instead of growing a culture, expanding socioeconomics, and building greater overall wealth.

I once worked with a gentleman in San Diego who's personally donated $8 million out of his own money to these causes. I asked him what foundation structure he had. He had figured this out by the time he had given his first million. He merged his organization with an educational organization and keeps record of the statistics: What is the average age at which the beneficiaries reproduce? Are they becoming self-sufficient? What are their educational levels? He has kept records and is making sure that he's producing a culture and not generating dependents. It is essential that the beneficiaries learn how to produce a product or service, to be commercial, and to sell and become self-sufficient. This gentleman does not just feed people without educating them in such a way that they can produce a commodity that can be sold locally, in their environment. He's helping build a more sustainable culture. He's building inspiration, not desperation.

As we've already seen, it's not wise to rescue desperation. Instead, it is wiser to invest in building an inspiring culture. Otherwise you'll just increase the population of insufficiency. The greater the population that costs more than they produce, the more that culture is declining. But as education and culture grow, the population growth slows down and productivity goes up.

In short, it's wise to investigate the charity rather than giving randomly. It's also wise to give anonymously, after you've investigated the charity and made sure it doesn't rob people of dignity, accountability, responsibility, and productivity. If you can't give anonymously, see it not as a charity but as a form of marketing.

Tithing

Tithe means *10 percent*. Tithing originates from extremely ancient cultures. When humans started having communal societies, people started to specialize in different types of work. Some jobs are not suitable for the aged, and some people are not able to be in the workforce, because children can't work until they're at least two. Consequently there's an average 7 percent of a population that won't be noticeably productive. The society knows that it must set aside what used to be called the "first fruits of the fields." They knew that they needed to support the 7 percent of the population that wasn't working or producing. They needed to have a 7 percent reserve and a 3 percent damage factor. They put 10 percent into a food reserve to take care of the people that couldn't work. They also had to set aside reserves to protect the society in case of devastation, insects, floods, and other natural disasters. So the society organized a tithing process and later taxes.

When organized religion, society, and state were merged together into a sort of theocracy, they started to collect that 10 percent into what was called a spiritual tithe or social tax. There's no universal law that says you have to take 10 percent, except that, as I've noted, people can tolerate 10 percent fluctuations without reacting and it takes about that amount to sustain a stable sociospiritual structure.

14

Walt Whitman at the Newspaper

No doubt you have heard of the great nineteenth-century American poet Walt Whitman.

When he was a boy, as one story goes, his dream was to be a writer. Originally he wanted to write for newspapers. One day when he was around twelve years old, he went to a newspaper and asked if he could talk to somebody about a job. They said, "You're just a child."

"Well," he said, "I'd like to talk to the manager about getting a job here. I'd like to work for the newspaper."

"You're too young, and there are no openings anyway."

"It's my dream to work for the newspaper. You don't have to pay me. I just want to work here."

So Walt went to the head office and talked to the manager. The manager said, "So you just want to work here? If that's what you want, we'll find you a little job here."

So the manager got Walt sweeping. He was running around, sweeping the place, and he really did the job thoroughly. He made sure to get into the crevices and in between the printing presses. At the same time, he was introducing himself to the reporters, writers, and typesetters.

Everybody loved Walt, because he was so enterprising, friendly, and hardworking. He interacted with people, and that was the most important part. He would inspire them just by his enterprising nature.

One day on his lunch break, he went over to where the writers were putting the articles for the paper together and said, "Do you mind if I just look over your shoulders and learn how you write? I want to be a writer someday."

Later on, Walt said to one of the writers, "Sir, I've dreamed about being a writer. Do you think that if I was to write something someday, you would take the time to read it and give me feedback, so I could be a writer like you?"

"Of course, Walt, of course. Just write away."

Walt started writing little essays and he'd give it to this writer. Finally the writer said, "You know, Walt, you're getting pretty astute at writing. This is actually a nice little piece. I'd like you to keep writing like that. And if you write something that I think I can use, maybe I can weave that into one of the articles here at the paper."

Encouraged, Walt continued to write away. He wrote a piece that the writer felt was worthy of being published. Even though it was under the other writer's name, he became known around the newspaper as the one who had written part of the article. That encouraged him to write another one. There was more reinforcing feedback, so the writer started using Walt to write more articles.

Finally, the news leaked out to the manager, who said, "I'm hearing, Walt, that you're the one that's actually writing some of the articles we are publishing, and we think that more papers are being sold because of them."

The manager could see that the increased sales had a lot to do with Walt's articles, so he gave him the opportunity to participate in writing more articles (still at no pay). He started to write more and longer articles, until finally he got to put his name on them. He got to be one of the writers, but still without pay. He was becoming known.

The manager finally said to him, "Walt, I can see that you're you've got a future in this business. My boy, just keep writing away, and someday you're going to be a great writer."

Walt kept writing and influencing more people. One day Walt felt that it was time to step up. During his lunch hour, he walked a number of blocks over to the competing newspaper and said, "I'd like to meet with a manager and talk about seeing if there happens to be a writing job opportunity."

The manager said, "You're a young man. We don't have any opportunities."

"I have been working at another newspaper, and my name is Walt Whitman."

The manager froze. "Walt Whitman. Haven't I seen that name? You're the writer for that other newspaper. Is that right?"

"Yes."

"Walt, my boy, it's interesting that you mentioned that. Just the other day when I was reading your column, I was saying, 'Boy, I wish I had a Walt like that working for our newspaper.' Yes, sir. I'll give you a job. In fact, I'll give you your own assistant, and I'll even pay you," and he named a certain amount.

"My God, sir, this is wonderful. Thank you so much. I think out of fairness, I need to go over to the other newspaper I presently work for and let them know I'll be leaving."

"Yes, sir. That's a very honorable thing to do; you go right ahead and do that. We'll have your office ready for you, and you can start fresh as soon as you want."

As Walt walked over to the other paper, he was anxious, thinking, "What am I going to say when I get over there? They've helped me so much."

Walt went back to his original newspaper and told the manager, "Sir, I want to let you know that I will be leaving the newspaper soon. I have been offered an opportunity at another newspaper, and they've offered me a paid position to write for them, as well as an assistant."

"Walt, wait a minute. You're a part of the family. You've been here from the beginning. This is your home. It's interesting you said this, because just the other day, my other buddy over here was thinking, 'It's time for Walt to get paid for his position.' What did they offer you over there?"

Walt told them the amount.

"Oh," said the manager, "we were going to do that at the beginning. We were going to give you opportunities to get beyond that. What else did they offer you?"

"A private assistant."

"We'll give you a private assistant, and we'll give you your own office and anything else. We'll match whatever they offer and give you more, because we don't want you to leave. This is your home, boy."

"Yes, sir. That really would be incredible. Now I don't know what to do, because I just told them I would be coming over there, and now you're offering me that amount and more. I guess I'll have to go back over to the other newspaper and tell them I won't be going over there after all. Let me go; it's a point of honor to tell them."

Walt then went back to the second newspaper and told them about the other offer. They raised the ante. He went back to the first newspaper and said, "They've offered this now."

"Well, then, we'll offer this."

Finally, Walt received much more income than any other writer in the newspaper.

What is the point of this story? A worthy being can certainly find or create a great job or build a career. Somebody who believes in themselves can find a way to make a great living by serving people and can begin to build financial wealth. They're willing to demonstrate their abilities. When someone really wants a job and to be of great service, they will do whatever it takes to get that job and will prove that they are worthy of it. There's no lack of income or money for resourceful people. There's simply somebody who hasn't accessed somebody else's highest value system and figured out how to provide a service according to their highest values or dominant buying motives. If they do, people will give up their fortunes for them.

People will pay you or do acts of service for you if you can provide something that inspires them in terms of their highest values. They will go out of their way to help you in ways that you never imagined. There's plenty of money in the world. If someone has serving human beings and financial wealth on the top of their values list, they will perceive the many financial opportunities already present around them. They be willing to do whatever it takes to give their services in a way that other people will value.

There is no lack of financial opportunities and potential income. If you feel that there is, you may not be taking advantage of the many opportunities. So go around and ask to be of service and then ask for referrals once you have "wowed" them. You may not be refining yourself and asking, "How can I serve ever greater numbers of people, and how can I refine my service until it is the finest?" You may not be going the extra mile or figuring out how to sell new services by caring about serving people enough to make the effort. If it is not truly high on your list of values, you probably won't.

When you can't wait to be of service, people can't wait to receive your service. Money will be there, waiting to come into your hands. It is waiting for you to care enough to serve. It's very helpful to be willing to take the action steps that most people aren't willing to take. When you become truly awakened to your inspired mission of service, you will do whatever it takes to fulfill it. Once you have a clear vision, a big enough reason, and a will to fulfill it, you will persist and achieve it. When there is a will, there's a way. When the why is big enough, the hows take care of themselves.

15
In Sum

Although I began with nine major points about building financial wealth, let me conclude by fleshing them out with a summary of many of the other chief ideas I've attempted to convey.

1. It's wise to appreciate the specialized skills, talents, or knowledge you have to offer others and to dedicate your energies to solving problems that serves them in ways they value enough to be willing to pay for.

2. One purpose of wealth building is to increase the opportunities in your life and those of other people.

3. Your hierarchy of values dictates your financial destiny. Shifting your hierarchy of values will shift your financial destiny.

4. If you continue doing what you're doing, you will continue to get what you have already gotten. It is up to you to make a shift in your financial destiny.

5. There's no legitimate reason not to begin saving, investing, and building your own business, financial fortune, and freedom.

6. Forced, automatic, and progressively accelerated saving and investing is a great starting point.

7. Wealthy people pay themselves first. Isn't it about time you started doing that today and becoming wealthy?

8. Wealth building is most viable and fruitful when you follow a strategy. In this book, I have given you a financial strategy that is clear and simple enough to follow.

9. A meaningful cause greater than yourself not only inspires you but inspires other people to help you in your pursuit of building fair, sustainable service and expanding financial reward.

10. It's wise to develop a series of savings and investment cushions in your financial house, so if you temporarily have what at first appears to be a setback, it's never too much or too far.

11. The quality of your financial life is based on the quality of the questions you ask yourself.

12. There is no shortage of ways to get handsomely or beautifully paid for doing what you love, so begin contemplating how.

13. By the inch, it's a cinch. Piggy banks become biggy banks. Build unstoppable financial momentum.

14. It is not so much about the amount saved or invested initially; it is about the habit, since the amount will continue to grow.

In Sum 251

15. The key is to find the service that inspires you and provide it in a way that you and those you serve are loved and appreciated for doing so.
16. When you manage your emotions wisely, you can begin to manage your money wisely.
17. It's wise to create a financial wealth building statement or affirmation that you are clear about and that truly inspires you and to recite it to yourself every single day.
18. When you have a high enough value on financial wealth building and your financial objectives truly align with your highest values, spontaneous fortunes begin to unfold.
19. To those who have, more is given; to those who have not, more is taken away, so pay yourself first and begin to have.
20. Convert your debt into service; then focus on the service so the debt goes away.
21. Moderate diversification reduces risk and stabilizes volatility.
22. Financial stressings are actually blessings that refine your financial wealth building actions into mastery.
23. Seeing whatever happens financially along the way as on the way and not in the way helps you build financial momentum that become unstoppable.
24. It's wise to not try to get something for nothing or to give something for nothing, for neither are fair exchanges or sustainable.
25. It is more productive to invest in inspiration than to rescue desperation.

26. Be not a lender without strict specifications about terms, amounts, and dates of repayment.

27. You will increase your wealth more efficiently and with greater certainty if you are patient with your savings and investments and transcend the temptation of trying to get rich quick.

28. Whoever has the most certainty in their financial management generates or attracts the most financial wealth.

29. It's wise to organize your financial house, prioritize your life, shed distractions, and delegate things that are less important to you.

30. If you have more energy at the end of the day than when you started, you know you've been inspired. If you have less energy at the end of the day, you know you've been uninspired.

31. You become independently wealthy by focusing on your primary, active source of income, savings, and investments, until your secondary, passive source of income exceeds your primary source.

32. If you give to a true culture building charity, you will have the most sustainable and rewarding results by donating anonymously.

33. If you help other people grow their culture, you become cultivated and financially rewarded.

34. Why would you expect others to invest in you until you invest in yourself?

35. The world around you is waiting for you to declare your financial worth, because when you value yourself, so does the world.

36. Gratitude expands your financial opportunities. If you appreciate what you have, you will receive more to appreciate.

37. Taxes are an important responsibility, but it is wise and legitimate to figure out how to reduce your taxes legally without evading them.

38. Your presentation will enhance your performance, so dress to achieve your financial aim.

What Else Could You Do in Your Life?

Taking the time to design a sound financial wealth building plan is wise and will pay off. Years ago, a famous study at Harvard showed that people with specific written goals went much farther than those that didn't. So live by design rather than surviving by duty. Money flows to financial houses that are highly ordered.

We still have remains of the great Egyptian pyramids some nearly 5,000 years after they were built. You can see that the masters behind these efforts had depth, vision, and inspiration. It's certainly worthwhile to study how they accomplished those achievements and realize, "What else could I do in my life?"

I wondered once, what else can I do that serves and that is possible? There is a famous quote from sociologist Margaret Mead: "Never underestimate the power of a small group of committed people to change the world. In fact, it is the only thing that ever has." I thought, "Why I couldn't be one of those people? If Newton can explore the grand divine design of the universe, so can I. If Bill Gates can become a billionaire by making a great contribution, so can I."

It's just as possible for you. They were human beings. Like everyone else, they had twenty-four hours in a day. They had the capacity to think, but they learned how to use their thinking. They may have had voids that drove inspiring values, but everybody has these if they look deeply enough into themselves.

It's a matter of finding your own magnificence and shining. Owning your magnificent contribution is part of wealth building, because self-worth and net worth often go together. You will grow your net worth if you grow your self-worth, and your self-worth has a lot to do with honoring your most authentic self and your magnificence—not exaggerating or minimizing yourself, but embracing your true profoundness. As Marianne Williamson wrote, "Our deepest fear is not that we are inadequate. Our deepest fear is that we are powerful beyond measure. It is our light, not our darkness that most frightens us." We don't serve the world by shrinking; we serve the world by shining.

Wealth building and freedom are so important that our culture depends on them. Cultural stability is based on the management and stability of that culture's wealth. Since financial wealth originally started out as well-being— which is really the self-actualization of an authentic inspired state—it's part of our inspired mission to master the art of wealth building. We are slaves if we don't, masters if we do.

There's absolutely no reason why one year from now, you can't be far financially wealthier than you are today.

Ten years or less from now, you could have your passive income far exceeding your normal active income and can achieve financial freedom. I'd like to be able to meet you ten years from now, if not before, and celebrate that achievement together.

Let's make that our dream. You can visualize how you would love your life to be, and you don't need let anybody or anything on this planet stop you from your dreams of building the financial wealth that you desire and deserve. I'll look forward to meeting you once you are even farther along your financial freedom adventure.

About the Author

D
r. John Demartini is a human behavioral specialist and founder of the Demartini Institute, a private research and education institute dedicated to activating leadership and human potential. He's an international best-selling author and business consultant, working with CEOs of Fortune 500 companies, celebrities, and sports personalities. Globally, he's worked with individuals and groups across many markets, including entrepreneurs, financiers, psychologists, teachers, and young adults, assisting and guiding them to greater levels of achievement, fulfillment, and empowerment in many areas of their lives.

For more information about Dr. John Demartini, his live events, and products and services, contact the Demartini Institute on info@drdemartini.com. To view his website, visit www.drdemartini.com.

www.ingramcontent.com/pod-product-compliance
Lightning Source LLC
Jackson TN
JSHW011357130125
77033JS00023B/721